52 MONDAYS

The One Year
Path to Outrageous Success
& Lifelong Happiness

_____

Vic Johnson

Laurenzana Press

Published by:

Laurenzana Press

PO Box 1220

Melrose, FL 32666 USA

www.LaurenzanaPress.com

✶✶✶✶

ISBN-13: 978-1-937918-71-2

**Watch The FREE Video 7 Simple Ways
To Make Every Monday Marvelous!**

My52Mondays.com

Contents

INTRODUCTION
A LOT CAN HAPPEN IN A YEAR

What have you done since this same time last year? Chances are you can think of many new life lessons, mistakes, victories and losses, because **a lot can happen in a year**.

In my case there have been a number of times when a year made a *huge* difference. For instance, in 1997 I had a family of five to support on just $14,027, but 365 days later I was earning a six-figure income. (For the doubting Thomases, I'm happy to supply a copy of my tax returns, since truth can be stranger than fiction!)

In 2002 I wanted to attract the woman of my dreams. I even went so far as to write down all the qualities I wanted her to possess. One year later I met my Proverbs 31 love of my life, and married her five years later in a storybook wedding (you can see the YouTube video at bit.ly/vicandlisa)

The 1991 World Series was chosen by ESPN as the "Greatest of All Time." But both teams who played for that championship – the Minnesota Twins and the Atlanta Braves – had both finished *last* in the preceding year. Up until that time no team who finished last the previous year made it to the Series the next year, and here were two who had gone from worst to first!

A lot *can* happen in a year, which is very important to remember as you begin this journey with me.

Now ask yourself, if you had started something new and worked on it every week since one year ago, what might you have been able to accomplish? Twelve months, after all, is plenty of time to start accruing success.

For example:

- If you had written 1,000 words every week, you'd be close to completing a novel. Or you could have published several how-to eBooks.

- If you had taken in one music lesson per week, you might be approaching a level of proficiency.

- If you had taken one day per week to start a side business, you could be entertaining the possibility of quitting your job.

If you've ever seen the 1994 movie "The Shawshank Redemption" (warning: spoilers ahead) you know Andy Dufresne (Tim Robbins) understood the geologic concept of pressure over time. Red (Morgan Freeman) said in a voiceover, "That's all it takes really: pressure and time." Red wasn't talking about geology; he was talking about Andy tunneling his way out of the prison over 20 years, getting rid of one pocket full of dirt at a time.

This guide isn't about working towards your goals, as that should be a given. It's about utilizing one year – just 52 weeks – to overcome your fear of failure and achieving success.

Remember: A successful person is still working on their previous New Year's resolutions by the time December 31st rolls around. Of course, committing a year to what you want to achieve isn't the easiest thing to do as it takes lots of patience. But if you have the fortitude and persistence and do your due diligence, the world will be your oyster!

**IMPORTANT: You Don't Have To Wait
Until The First of the Year**

One of the most important goals I ever achieved was one that I started on in OCTOBER. It doesn't have to be the first of the year, the first of the month or even the first of the week.

There's no magic about when you start. The magic is in getting started!

And there's no problem starting this book anytime of the year and progressing week by week.

So let's start with Monday number one to show you how you're going to achieve your New Year's resolutions, and make this coming year one you'll always be proud of!

* * *

(**Attention All Eagle Eyes:** We've had a number of people proof this book before we released it to you, but there is a chance you might spot something that was missed. If you find a typo or other obvious error please send it to us. And if you're the first one to report it, <u>we'll send you a free gift</u>! Send to: corrections@laurenzanapress.com)

MONDAY 1
NUMBER

Monday number one is the single-most important day for succeeding, since this is the day you'll define your criteria for success and choose the path you're going to be traveling. It's more important than ever to follow through on the promises you made on New Year's Eve when ruminating on what you want to accomplish in the upcoming year.

The next 52 Mondays will be about properly managing your time, since there is nothing more wasteful than putting things off for another day. How many times have you said "I'll get to it tomorrow"? Just in case you don't fully understand the impact of this statement, pay close attention: All you get in this life are an endless sequence of "todays" as **there is no guarantee for the future**.

That's great if you've already established your goals for the year as you know where you're going to spend your energy. But if you haven't taken that first step, you need to think about what you're willing to commit to over the next 52 weeks.

If you decide to take one small step each day (such as making a phone call to a prospective client, or sending out an email), that's fine. But if you can knock out those steps five or ten minutes after you get out of bed – which will leave time to enjoy the rest of your day – even better!

The point is that week one is about establishing *momentum* for a full year. Imagine that success is a large boulder sitting precariously on the top of a hill. If you give it a gentle nudge, it might roll a bit but won't make it all the way down the hill. All that's required of you this week is that you give your "boulder" a little shove every day, so that when next Monday comes it will be a little further down the hill. And by the end of 52 weeks, you'll be happy that it successfully reached its goal of nestling at the bottom of the hill.

Throughout the next year you're going to realize that you and you alone stopped the pursuit of your dreams. So come on … now is the time to be enthusiastic about this exciting new phase of your life!

Exercise 1: Choose a Method to Keep you Motivated

You may have heard the saying, "Yesterday, you said 'tomorrow.'" Don't let that be you! Every day you need to remind yourself that today is *the* day to make a change.

Whether you want to lose weight, write a screenplay or a novel, or start an online business, you need to find methods to keep yourself motivated and accountable. So your assignment this week is to choose at least one of the accountability methods mentioned below and get it in place before the end of the week:

- Join an online support group (TheChampionsClub.org is a great place to start). Make at least one friend, set your goal, and structure how you're going to record your daily efforts.

- Post a note where you'll see it first thing in the morning and right before bed. Some suggested spots are the bathroom mirror, the coffee maker or the fridge – somewhere prominent where you can't miss it. Write a statement of "Today I will…" that moves you one step closer to your goal. Then after you've accomplished it that day, take it down before you go to bed. Repeat it the next morning. Keep a goals journal of the steps you achieved so you can review your accomplishments throughout the year.

- Find someone (maybe from your support group) who wants to achieve the same goal as much or more than you do, and make a pact to check in with each other every day. Choose the format you'll use such as email, text, phone, shared drop box, or in person to keep you both accountable.

- Hire someone to keep you on task such as a life coach, personal trainer, mentor or a group leader (such as a sponsor through AA, or programs that support the obstacles you have).

Remember:

- You're a champion every day and in every way. You know it and every one around you knows it.

- Today, nothing can stand in your way.

- When you need extra determination, you've got it!

- When you need more energy and drive, you've got it!

- You've got the power to get anything done and the patience to overcome challenges, no matter what they may be.

- You can do this and you know you can!

MONDAY 2
NUMBER

Last week I wanted to nudge you in the right direction by giving you few steps to get you in the habit of following through on your goals. This week more will be expected of you, as I want you to become aware of your thoughts.

Remember last week when I told you that you're the greatest obstacle to your success? Well, thoughts are some of the most powerful tools you'll have at your disposal to overcome those obstacles. Thoughts create feelings … feelings create actions … and actions create results. In fact, thoughts are so closely related to action that you can consider action as a form of "physical thought."

The biggest challenge to changing the way you think is when you're faced with something negative and you don't know how to feel good about it. For example, how can you have a "find money" mindset if bills keep showing up in your mailbox? Or how can you have a "fitness" mindset if you look in the mirror and only see those pesky ten pounds in your muffin top?

You'll be surprised at how reframing your thoughts can change everything. Let's say you're faced with a stack of bills, and your goal throughout the year is to make more money to pay them off. You'll find it impossible to change your thoughts to a "wealthy" mindset if all you see is money flying out the window.

But at this point you don't have to think "I'm wealthy"; you just need to make a small shift in your thought process. You can ask questions like "What if I were wealthy?" Or "What if I had the capacity to overcome the obstacles keeping me from being wealthy?" Questions instead of statements have the advantage of not intruding on your internal "lie detector." You know when you're lying to yourself, but when you ask a question you're being nothing but honest.

Then you need to find a way to resolve your questions such as:

- What would I do if I were wealthy?

- How would I act if I had the capacity to overcome my obstacles?

- What would I do if I were unstoppable?

- What would this week be like if I decide to act that way?

Exercise 2: The Power of the Calendar

It's not enough to dream about your goals: You need to plan even the tiniest steps it takes to achieve them. This week you'll need to invest in a 12-month calendar (you need a paper one so you can put it somewhere in plain sight), then start dreaming. Write down your goal at the end of the year, then set monthly benchmarks to keep you focused.

Be very specific. For example, if you want to lose 40 pounds by the end of the year you'll need to divide it by 12 months. Then mark your benchmark weight (40 ÷ 12 = 3.33), exercise and dietary goals at the beginning of each month.

Maybe your goal is to start an online business. Set a monetary goal for the end of the year, and come up with a business plan for the next 12 months such as setting benchmarks for the end of each month in terms of business contacts, website development, how much you need to make each month, etc.

Post the calendar somewhere you can see it each day, and make notes about your progress. Tell your accountability partner you chose in week one about your calendar exercise, and encourage them to do the same.

Remember:

- You're a champion every day and in every way. You know it and every one around you knows it.

- Today, nothing can stand in your way.

- When you need extra determination, you've got it!

- When you need more energy and drive, you've got it!

- You've got the power to get anything done and the patience to overcome challenges, no matter what they may be.

- You can do this and you know you can!

MONDAY
NUMBER 3

Two things have been established so far: Your actions and thoughts. During week one you took baby steps toward your goal. During the second week you learned how to make a shift in your thinking that will lead to a shift in your actions.

Your "boulder" should be rolling a little easier by now in week three. But you've got to keep pushing it if you want to end up at a better place by the end of the year. So for this week you're going to focus on taking action by establishing habits.

Aristotle said, "We are what we *repeatedly* do." If you stopped your actions last week, you would have quit at about the same time most people give up on their New Year's resolutions, which is why you're going to momentarily digress to reframe your actions into habits during week three.

During week one you considered what types of actions you could take every day to achieve your goal. But now you need to change and/or create habits in order to improve those results for the rest of the year. Creating new habits isn't easy, especially if you're trying to chuck a meaningless habit as your mind is wired to find stability in your life.

But you can shake things up, even if your mind tries to get you back into old habits after day one. Remember that you're your worst obstacle and will be all year if you can't switch gears.

Not doing it this week just means you'll have to start again next week (remember, there are only *todays*!).

This week you need to take a look at some habits you can change, such as what you eat for breakfast, the route you take to work in the morning, or how much television you watch at night.

Here's a point about establishing habits: If you decide to work out each morning, it's better to work out for just five minutes than to skip the day. You're a creature of habit, so which ones do you want to change this week?

Exercise 3: Establish One New Habit

You want to establish habits that are manageable and practical enough to get you closer to your goal. To jog your imagination, below are listed some suggestions of new ones to create:

- If you want to lose weight, commit to eating a low-calorie fruit or vegetable every meal.

- If you want to write a book, commit to writing 15 minutes or more each day.

- If you want a new job or want to move up in the company, commit to at least 15 minutes a day to developing the skills you'll need.

- If you want to start your own business, commit to a minimum of 15 minutes a day working on developing a business plan (website content, creating inventory for future sales, researching the steps for a start-up, etc.).

Celebrate every time you use your new habit by putting a smiley face on your calendar, reporting in to your accountability partner, or marking your success in an online forum or support website.

If you miss a day, reaffirm your commitment to the action and goal and keep going. If you don't take the scheduled action for three or more days, you need to give some serious thought about your desire to reach your goal. Was it scheduled for the wrong time of day? Was it as important to your achievement as you originally thought? Is the goal really something you want to commit to?

For a number of years I put on my goals list that I wanted to write a book. I tried to establish habits towards achieving that goal, but several years passed and I hadn't written even one chapter. I became discouraged and questioned my desire to write. But as time went on I realized the timing wasn't right, so I put it on a future goals list and tackled something else.

In 2003 the desire became so strong that nothing could hold me back, so I began to take steps to write my first book and completed it in less than 90 days. I'm proud to say I've sold more than 75,000 copies, and it's been translated into Japanese, Czech, Slovak and Farsi. Since then I've written five other books because I had created habits to make writing easier and quicker.

The same will be true for you and your goals, so you need to establish a new habit this week! Once you see how simple the process actually is, you'll be excited to see what the next 51 weeks can produce.

Remember:

- You're a champion every day and in every way. You know it and every one around you knows it.

- Today, nothing can stand in your way.

- When you need extra determination, you've got it!

- When you need more energy and drive, you've got it!

- You've got the power to get anything done and the patience to overcome challenges, no matter what they may be.

- You can do this and you know you can!

MONDAY
NUMBER 4

Last week was devoted to action and changing your habits, so now you need to refocus your thoughts.

Your thoughts are intensely private. But if I were able to read them, what would you be thinking? How many times would you forego doing something because you didn't know how to get started, you felt it was too difficult, or you didn't believe you could do it?

For many of people the answer would be embarrassing, as they would have no way to justify their actions. Which is why I keep pounding home the fact that <u>you</u> are your worst enemy! It's *your* thoughts alone that convince you you've failed. It's *your* thoughts, and no one else's, that sabotage your desire for success.

Napoleon Hill's classic self-help book, *Think and Grow Rich*, devotes an entire chapter to autosuggestion, which is the act of believing a lie you tell your subconscious.

When you go to the drive-through window instead of making something to eat for dinner, you're auto-suggesting it's easier and quicker to eat fast food than a healthy meal.

When you sit down to start writing your novel but a blank page stares back, you shut down the computer because you've auto-suggested you'll start again tomorrow, when you're just fooling yourself into thinking you can't write.

When you think *I can't do it*, is that the message you want your subconscious to hear?

That's doubtful. So let's concentrate on changing your need to sabotage your actions by changing the way you think.

Affirmations (or autosuggestions) are great tools, and there are a few important things you should know how to utilize them:

- They should be stated in the present tense: "My business is bringing clients in."

- They should be stated in the positive rather than the negative: "I am happy" is better than "I am not sad."

- They should be said with sincere emotion and intent.

- They should be written down so you can repeatedly refer to them. For instance, you can write them on index cards and carry them with you throughout the day.

Although the affirmations you pick should focus on the goal you chose at the beginning of the year, you should choose ones to help create the right "mental environment." Say your goal is to save $10,000 by the end of the year. At this point you might not be able to process "I have $10,000 in the bank" in the present tense, so you can try an affirmation like "I love to save money and I find new ways to save every day." Give this a try and see how much you've progressed by the time week five rolls around. As your belief grows you'll be able to adopt the $10,000 affirmation without doubting you can achieve it.

Exercise 4: Daily Affirmations

Choose an affirmation that highlights the habit you want to establish for the week. Then write it down and share it on your accountability board or with your accountability partner. Then post it on your calendar and anywhere you'll see it during the day.

Repeat the affirmation at least once every time you practice your new habit. For example, you could do any of the following:

- Tell yourself I am fit and strong as you work out.

- Tell yourself I like eating healthy food as you eat fruits and vegetables with each meal.

- Tell yourself I am a small business owner before you begin your research or new business plan.

- Tell yourself I love writing as you settle in to work on your screenplay or novel.

You get the idea.

Choose an affirmation that's easy to remember and use it to reinforce your new habit, which you'll continue to establish this week.

Remember:

- You're a champion every day and in every way. You know it and every one around you knows it.

- Today, nothing can stand in your way.

- When you need extra determination, you've got it!

- When you need more energy and drive, you've got it!

- You've got the power to get anything done and the patience to overcome challenges, no matter what they may be.

- You can do this and you know you can!

(BTW, in case you didn't realize it in the previous weeks, this is an example of an affirmation. And a very successful one at that. It's been used by thousands of achievers around the world!)

MONDAY 5
NUMBER

One month down, eleven to go and now it's crunch time. You may be thinking, *Already? Wouldn't that be more appropriate in November or December?* The answer is, not really. You see, many people give up their New Year's goals in January. But if you've made it this far, you've improved your odds of continuing to the end by a heckuva lot!

My wise friend Steve Siebold said, "Now is the time to get mentally tough." Whether you feel good about how far you've come or frustrated by the lack of results, the challenge is to keep going despite your subconscious telling you to hold on to old habits. Now that you've gotten into the habit of affirming new thoughts, you can change your affirmations to suit your needs.

For example, if you feel frustrated, state affirmatively that things *are* getting better (present tense) and that you know how to change your situation. If you feel like resting on your laurels, state affirmatively that you have renewed energy and enthusiasm for your goals.

Whatever the challenge, the purpose of this week remains the same: To continue the momentum you established in month one, which means you should stick with your new habits and affirmations. Never give up, no matter how much you may feel like it or how much easier it will seem.

Remember, the next 12 months will be an experiment with time, and you'll thank yourself *in spades* for the actions you take *this very week.*

Are you going to let you or your future down? Or are you going to make use of every opportunity you can in the present? The answer is up to you, as it's you who has to seize the initiative, boost yourself when you feel depressed, and keep pushing forward when you feel bogged down.

In the scheme of things one month isn't a lot of time, so don't feel bad if you haven't accomplished much at this point. The boulder on the top of the hill is slow to move at first, but at some point you'll give it one more shove and it will begin rolling on its own. **Believe it and it will happen**. So hang on, you're going to have a great week!

Exercise 5: Building Mental Toughness Muscles

This week you're going to challenge yourself to grow in mental toughness, which basically means sticktoitiveness or dogged perseverance.

Have you done the habit you chose in week three every day for the past two weeks? If your answer is yes, this exercise will have you add something small that challenges you mentally or physically. If your answer is no, you'll need to recommit to establishing the habit into your daily routine.

Talk to your accountability partner (or post your resolution on an accountability board or online forum), stating exactly what you're going to do each day and at what time.

Pick a reward for honoring your commitment each day, and set a punishment for skipping it even one day. The reward and punishment must be immediate and simple. For example, you might reward yourself with a favorite beverage immediately after completing the task. The punishment might be to confess your lack of commitment on your support forum when you don't follow through.

As you go through this exercise, remind yourself that you're mentally tough enough to establish this new habit. You have the discipline and the motivation to take the baby steps required to create change in your life.

Remember:

- You're a champion every day and in every way. You know it and every one around you knows it.

- Today, nothing can stand in your way.

- When you need extra determination, you've got it!

- When you need more energy and drive, you've got it!

- You've got the power to get anything done and the patience to overcome challenges, no matter what they may be.

- You can do this and you know you can!

MONDAY
NUMBER 6

Many steps in the self-help world get confused because people aren't paying attention to one single requisite principle of success. It's a short six-letter word, and once you understand its importance you'll never be the same again.

A-C-T-I-O-N

People who achieve a lot of success often do so as a result of taking *massive action*. Sure, they might have had a lot of other factors going their way – a positive attitude, their belief system, good genes and an inheritance, etc. But many factors either contribute to or are a result of taking positive action. And the more the better!

Jeff Bezos left his job on the East Coast and headed to Washington State to start Amazon.com. During the trip his wife drove while he was on the phone with potential investors, which was the reason why Amazon launched after **just 90 days of massive action**. If Bezos was willing to take that level of action, is there any doubt as to why Amazon is such a huge success?

After only one month of working towards your goals, you've achieved a new level of "normal" for how much action you take in your daily life. You've already got a plan, and you know what steps are needed to achieve your goal. But if you stay at that level and don't make any progress, your results will stay the same. Therefore, if you want to hyper-accelerate your results, it's time to crank the volume up as your mind can tolerate a lot more work.

I keep sticky note affirmations on my computer to keep them top-of-mind. A particularly favorite one is a quote by Robert Louis Stevenson: "Don't judge each day by the harvest you reap, but by the seeds that you plant," which reminds me that it's the seeds I plant today that will determine the harvest I have tomorrow.

Starting today, this week's exercise is to identify one step you need to take in order to reach your goal and dial the action to a higher level. Maybe you need to send out emails to prospective clients, so generate a list and email more clients today than you have in an entire week. Then do it again every day for the rest of the week.

By day seven, what are the results? How do you view yourself? Instead of feeling burned out, I'll wager that you're feeling energized and enthusiastic – more so than you have been in a very long time.

Massive action is a force of gravity that pulls all the other principles of success with it. You'll gain faith, energy, and motivation for greater achievement. So try it this week and push the boundaries of possibilities.

Exercise 6: Take a Risk

This week you're going to take a risk that will shake you out of your complacency. You'll examine your end goal and identify a risk that will both thrill and terrify you. This exercise is easy because you only have to do one thing. But it's harder than previous exercises in that it needs to be something that matters.

For example:

- If you dream of being toned and strong go to a climbing wall, or take a fitness class above your comfort level.

- If you want to get published participate in a writing club meeting, or perform at a poetry slam.

- If you want to be a musician, participate in an open mic night at a local club or coffeehouse.

- If you want to start your own business, cold call one potential client and pitch your services.

- If you want to start freelancing apply to one gig on Craigslist, Elance.com or Odesk.com.

- If you want to start dating go to a speed-dating event, or register online with a dating service.

The outcome doesn't really matter. You're succeeding *just by trying*. The lesson here is that taking a risk can bring great rewards, that failure isn't fatal, and that success is possible. So have fun!

Remember:

- You're a champion every day and in every way. You know it and every one around you knows it.

- Today, nothing can stand in your way.

- When you need extra determination, you've got it!

- When you need more energy and drive, you've got it!

- You've got the power to get anything done and the patience to overcome challenges, no matter what they may be.

- You can do this and you know you can!

MONDAY 7
NUMBER

Now that you've taken massive action to a higher level, you should feel more motivated.

But what if your enthusiasm and drive haven't risen as much as you thought they would? What do you need to do to take action energized with the vitality of self-confidence?

If the results of your actions fell a little flat last week, it's time to boost your enthusiasm. And you can start by remembering that you're taking massive action with a very big prize waiting for you at the end of the year: YOUR GOAL!

Ask yourself is the pleasure of having that goal worth the work you put in now? Of course it is, even if it's not immediately evident. Keep reminding yourself that this is a year-long process and isn't something that can be fixed overnight.

Your ultimate goal is to arrive at your desired location at the desired time. Would you go on a plane ride that's supposed to last two hours, then ask them to turn around when you hadn't arrived at your destination in 15 minutes? No, you wouldn't. Because you know you're going to land at the right airport at the right time, considering you're staying on course at the correct speed.

You need to take that same attitude with goal setting. You're on a plane ride for the next 11 months, so just stay on course and you'll eventually arrive at your destination.

But you're going to go off course and feel like you want to turn around if you don't stay energized or enthusiastic, which is what this week is all about.

It's okay to fantasize about your goals having been achieved (provided you don't use that as an excuse to quit). In fact, it's quite fine to use frustration as a way to add enthusiasm and energy to your action. If you're frustrated and feel bad, the way to overcome those negative feelings isn't to quit but to work even harder.

My wife and partner, Lisa, is the publisher of our MyDailyInsights.com, and she chooses quotes or stories to inspire and motivate our readers. One month she posted this quote by Muhammad Ali: "I hated every minute of training. But I said, 'Don't quit. Suffer now and live the rest of your life as a champion.'" I thought about the life Ali must have had as an international icon and the price he must have paid. The trials and tribulations and all his efforts were a huge bargain for his success as a Golden Gloves winner, Olympic medalist, and proud father. And it will be the same for you!

Exercise 7: Ten Ways Your Life Will Change

Take 30 minutes at the beginning of the week when you can commit 100% focus to this exercise.

First, write in detail ten ways your life will be changed for the better because of your efforts this year.

Second, evaluate them the same way Ali looked at his life, and how you're going to live life as a champion.

Lastly, make sure you revisit those ten points every day to remind yourself *why* you're paying the price now to be successful at the end of the year.

Remember:

- You're a champion every day and in every way. You know it and every one around you knows it.

- Today, nothing can stand in your way.

- When you need extra determination, you've got it!

- When you need more energy and drive, you've got it!

- You've got the power to get anything done and the patience to overcome challenges, no matter what they may be.

- You can do this and you know you can!

MONDAY 8
NUMBER

This week you need to ask yourself a very important question.

First, imagine having achieved your goal at the end of the year (i.e., a big promotion at work). Then ask yourself, *What kind of person did I need to become in order to achieve that goal?* The answer should be, *I needed to become the type of person who could achieve my goals.* (*Duh! That's what I've been trying to become all along!*)

But how honest are you being with yourself?

For example, if you want six-pack abs you're not just going to do crunches; you're going to have to *become* the person with six-pack abs. You'll have to change your diet to burn fat. You'll have to stay disciplined enough to keep working out. You'll have to do cardio and muscle work for extended periods of time. The subtle distinction is that your six-pack abs will be a result of **who you've become** to get those abs. Get it? Got it? Good!

Friend, mentor and motivational guru Jim Rohn said that people should become millionaires – not for the money, but for the people they become in the process.

So what kind of person do you need to be to accomplish your year-end goal? Are your actions congruous with an achiever? Or have you become undisciplined, unenergetic or lethargic? Have you been criticizing yourself? Your "prescription" for what ails you is for you to decide how you'll spend your time this week.

You can learn tools for developing the right habits from success and motivational books (heck, you're reading one right now!). But are you going to putter along in the car driving you to your goal, hoping the engine doesn't conk out? Or are you filling the tank, revving the engine, and driving like someone who's confident they're going to arrive at their correct destination?

This week I'm going to tell you to "**Make a great week**" instead of just "Have a good week." Trust me … by day seven you'll understand the difference.

Exercise 8: Tap Into Pleasurable Rewards

This week you need to think about what pleasures you'll experience when you reach your goal. Write them out in great detail, describing specifically what it will feel like to…

• Have more money

• Finish that project

• Own your own company

• Have a novel out to a publisher

• Have a new relationship

• Strut your stuff with confidence on the dance floor

• Cross the finish line (also a lovely metaphor for achieving your goal!)

Read these as you plan your day and every night before you go to sleep, making sure your schedule reflects the steps to achieve your goal.

To sweeten the deal, celebrate with a pleasurable reward each time you achieve a success. Eat a piece of expensive chocolate, luxuriate in a bubble bath, or enjoy a glass of your favorite wine.

You get the point. Enjoying pleasurable rewards as you dream about your end goal will make your success sweeter and more tangible!

Remember:

- You're a champion every day and in every way. You know it and every one around you knows it.

- Today, nothing can stand in your way.

- When you need extra determination, you've got it!

- When you need more energy and drive, you've got it!

- You've got the power to get anything done and the patience to overcome challenges, no matter what they may be.

- You can do this and you know you can!

MONDAY 9
NUMBER

"Monty Python's Flying Circus" used to transition by saying "...and now for something completely different," which seems appropriate for this ninth Monday.

This week I'm going to talk about the Universal Law of Gender that says everything has a gestation period (the length of time from birth to maturity). A seed of corn has a *physical* gestation period of 70 to 90 days; a human being nine months; and an elephant 22 months!

But goals and dreams have a *mental* gestation period. Failure to realize this simple fact is a source of unnecessary frustration and heartache for people who don't know why they aren't doing better in life. Considering that you've spent two months in the process to achieve your goals, it seems like an appropriate time to talk about *your* gestation period.

Mental gestation means the conception or development of an idea. Each goal has a different length of growth, and you never know when yours will blossom. Some people see results right away, while others have to chip away for a long time before their big break.

Did you grow a lima bean in a milk carton at school? Or plant a garden in your back yard? It took a while to see the little green plant poke its head through the dirt, didn't it? The point is just because you can't see the something above ground doesn't mean it's not growing underneath.

Take a moment to look at the bigger picture. It often takes **90 days** of massive action and sustained effort to see noticeable results of your efforts. So despite how far you've come these past three months, you're not quite there yet.

Patience is the name of the game. Most people give up way too early, and often when they're on the verge of succeeding. If you're approaching your goals with massive action on a regular basis, and changing your strategy and habits to overcome obstacles, there's nothing to do but to continue the process and wait.

You might ask, *What am I waiting for?* Well, it's still up in the air and it's still up to you. Maybe you're waiting for that ideal client to finally make a big purchase, but you didn't take action by dialing their number.

The key to patience is to keep reminding yourself that success is just around the corner. The seed *is* growing under the dirt. And if you stop now you may never see how close you were to seeing the result of your success.

To start you off this week, I'd like to share a portion of "Don't Quit" (author unknown), a poem I've carried with me for 30 years:

Life is queer with its twists and turns, As every one of us sometimes learns, And many a fellow turns about When he might have won had he stuck it out. Don't give up though the pace seems slow - You may succeed with another blow.

Often the goal is nearer than It seems to a faint and faltering man; Often the struggler has given up When he might have captured the victor's cup; And he learned too late when the night came down How close he was to the golden crown.

Success is failure turned inside out – The silver tint of the clouds of doubt, And you never can tell how close you are, It may be near when it seems afar; So stick to the fight when you're hardest hit - It's when things seem worst that you must not quit.

Exercise 9: Envision Success

This week you're going to become an artist. Pick up a poster board and some basic art supplies, then go home and create a collage that symbolizes your success. Fill the collage with things such as…

• Words that describe your success

• Happy photos of you

• Pictures of things that represent your success (from magazines, the internet, etc.)

Then prop your collage somewhere you can see it often. Go ahead and laugh if it looks amateurish. It doesn't matter how aesthetically pleasing your artwork is; what counts is you're implanting a clear vision of who you will become once you succeed.

Then look at your collage at the beginning of the week, and while working towards your goal throughout the week.

Remember:

• You're a champion every day and in every way. You know it and every one around you knows it.

- Today, nothing can stand in your way.

- When you need extra determination, you've got it!

- When you need more energy and drive, you've got it!

- You've got the power to get anything done and the patience to overcome challenges, no matter what they may be.

- You can do this and you know you can!

MONDAY
NUMBER 10

This week I have a very important question for you to ask yourself: *If I knew I could never achieve my goal, would I still pursue it?* You might answer, *Of course I wouldn't. What would be the point of all this hard work if don't succeed?*

There's a very enlightened way of adopting the kind of mindset that will keep you from quitting, even when times are tough and you want to give up. And that is working toward your goal should be in and of itself worth the time you commit, the pain you experience, and the rewards you receive today.

Think about someone training for a marathon. They have an end goal in mind, but they know they have to train a long time before they can reach that goal, so they run and run and run … and run.

You might ask how could a human being experience that much sacrifice and pain for one fleeting moment of achievement? The answer is it's not just for one moment – it's for all the benefits they get from running on a daily basis. Sure, they get a runner's high while training, and feel more energized at the end of the marathon. But they also feel proud when they go to bed for even their smallest of accomplishments, and are rewarded with a good night's rest.

You need to focus on the little rewards and benefits that make success worth it *even if you never achieve your goal.* This doesn't mean you should ignore your goal; you just need to keep readjusting your strategies to make sure you're still aiming for it, and use it as motivation to keep you energized during your journey.

You also need to realize that if you don't take every day's action seriously, you'll probably end up quitting. Once you get to the point of taking today's action for today's sake, you'll be set free and you'll fly!

You've probably heard more than one successful person say the journey was more enjoyable and valuable than the final achievement. Jim Rohn said, "The major reason for setting a goal is for what it makes of you to accomplish it. What it makes of you will always be the far greater value than what you get."

So this week take enough action every day so you can feel proud of what you've done. Then ask yourself if it was enjoyable enough that you want to keep doing it all year. I think we both know what the answer will be.

Exercise 10: Enjoy the Process

This week your exercise is to identify one piece of the process you enjoy and indulge in it as you pursue your goals. For example, you might:

- Thoroughly enjoy your post-run shower

- Feel proud when you order a salad at lunch

- Really love designing your new website, or the logo for your new company

- Laugh at yourself when writing your blogposts, and create a "best of"

- Enjoy online flirting

- Shop for business attire for your meeting with a venture capitalist

Have fun with your goal setting this week. You deserve it!

Remember:

- You're a champion every day and in every way. You know it and every one around you knows it.

- Today, nothing can stand in your way.

- When you need extra determination, you've got it!

- When you need more energy and drive, you've got it!

- You've got the power to get anything done and the patience to overcome challenges, no matter what they may be.

- You can do this and you know you can!

MONDAY

You're 11 Mondays into the program, which means you should have learned something about persistence. But 11 Mondays does not a lifetime of achievement make.

Here's a great story of ultimate persistence. In 1966, Maxcy Filer took the California Bar exam for the first time at age 36, far later than most fresh out of law school graduates attorneys usually do. But he failed.

He took it again. And he failed again. He took it again and again and again, and kept failing each time.

So he decided to change his strategy and started taking it in different locations such as Los Angeles, San Diego, Riverside, San Francisco and anywhere else it was offered.

And he failed each time.

He took the exam when his children were young. And eventually when his two sons went to law school and started their own practice, he took it with them. But he continued to fail.

After 25 years, $50,000 spent in exam fees and review courses, and 144 days in testing rooms, Maxcy Filer took the exam for the 48th – yes, 48th! – time and passed it at the age of 61.

Maxcy had so many failures that he could have quit and tried something else. When he changed his strategy by taking the tests all across California, nothing changed. But he persisted, resolving never to give up in order to prevent an end-of-life story about what "could have been."

Half of Maxcy's life wasn't about achieving his dream, but simply to get on the path of becoming a lawyer by passing the state bar exam. If that's the kind of perseverance and patience Maxcy could have for his goals, then how much have you achieved by your 11th Monday?

This doesn't discount the work you've achieved and patience you've shown in getting this far. The further you go, the more unique your own story will become. But it does help keep things in perspective.

John Lennon said, "Life is what happens to you while you're busy making other plans."

Enjoy your life every day, proud of the knowledge that you're not giving up on reaching your goal. Persistence meant success for Maxcy Filer, and it'll mean success for you as well!

Exercise 11: Get Inspired

- Research someone who has done exactly what you hope to accomplish; or something you find inspiring that's just as hard, if not harder, to accomplish.

- Buy a biography about this person.

- Set aside 15 minutes before bed each night to read the book.

- Or listen to the audiobook as you commute to work.

- Find a photo of this person (or something that symbolizes their achievements) and put it on your collage.

Celebrating another person's achievements will inspire you to achieve. In addition, learning from their mistakes will give you insight to spare you unnecessary pain and setbacks.

Start thinking of yourself as equal to this person. They're a human being just like you, right? They put on pants one leg at a time, and they need to eat, sleep and work hard just like you do. If they can do it, so can you!

Remember:

- You're a champion every day and in every way. You know it and every one around you knows it.

- Today, nothing can stand in your way.

- When you need extra determination, you've got it!

- When you need more energy and drive, you've got it!

- You've got the power to get anything done and the patience to overcome challenges, no matter what they may be.

- You can do this and you know you can!

MONDAY NUMBER 12

You're almost three months into the program. If you've made it this far while keeping your eye on the prize, pat yourself on the back for having a great deal of patience and determination.

Week 12 is about giving you a visual boost that will light the way for the rest of your journey.

In 1987, a relatively unknown 25-year-old actor, Jim Carrey, drove his Toyota up to Mulholland Drive and high up in the Hollywood Hills. He went there to look at the vista of Los Angeles, and to dream about what could be in his future. He was frustrated that things weren't going the way he'd hoped, but he wasn't ready to throw in the towel.

That's when he came up with the idea of writing himself a check for $10 million, and dated it "Thanksgiving 1995" with a note "For acting services rendered." He stuck the check in his wallet, and every time frustration would set in he'd pull it out, stare at it, and connect with all of his emotions about what the check really represented.

I don't have to tell you that not only did Jim Carrey's dream come true, but he exceeded his wildest expectations by setting a new benchmark for salaries in Hollywood. By the time Thanksgiving 1995 rolled around, he wasn't making $10 million per movie … he was making $20 million! Today, Jim Carrey has had a long career of being one of Hollywood's most beloved actors. Quite an accomplishment for someone who, in 1987, could have been described as a down-on-his-luck dreamer.

Business coach and motivational speaker, Brian Tracy, says that all successful people are dreamers. They start with the dream and then work backwards, filling in the blanks as they go along.

That's what I want you to be!

You need to find some way to make your dream – the goal you want to achieve by the end of your 52 Mondays – prominent as a constant reminder for where you want to be. It doesn't have to be in the form of a check, but it can be if that kind of visualization works for you.

You need to come up a visual aid that means a great deal to you. Be a dreamer, look at that reminder every time you feel like giving up, and ask yourself, *What can I do today to make that real in the future?*

Of course it will take some sort of sacrifice. You might have to do something today that isn't your concept of fun. Heck, even marathon runners can't admit they like running *all* the time. They're tired, hungry and sweaty, but they know what it takes to win.

A visual reminder will keep you on task for 52 Mondays, and you won't mind the work you have to do today to get to the end. Plus, if you are a dreamer maybe part of you *does* like the sacrifice. Now, there's the sweet spot!

Exercise 12: Make a Move that Requires Faith

This week you need to make a commitment that requires faith in yourself and your goal. For example, you could:

• Book a week at a writing conference or retreat.

- Pay for an ad that announces the opening of your business.

- Sign up for a mentoring program that requires a long-term commitment.

- Register for a class reunion even if you haven't lost the weight you want.

- Sign up for a race beyond your comfort level.

Once you've made a commitment, you'll need to assess your progress. Are you sticking with your new habit, or have you backed out? Did you book your flight and hotel room for the conference? Did you pay for the ad? Have you met the person you'll be mentoring? Did you go shopping for new clothes for the reunion? Have you started training for the race?

Check in with your accountability partner or program to make sure you're on track to meet your goal.

Remember:

- You're a champion every day and in every way. You know it and every one around you knows it.

- Today, nothing can stand in your way.

- When you need extra determination, you've got it!

- When you need more energy and drive, you've got it!

- You've got the power to get anything done and the patience to overcome challenges, no matter what they may be.

- You can do this and you know you can!

MONDAY
NUMBER 13

Thus far, everything's been focused on your goals, your dreams, and the action you'll need to take to get where you want. If, however, you've reached a plateau, don't fret as this chapter might just have the answer for kick-starting you back into gear.

You may have heard "The more you give, the more you get." Or "you reap what you sow." In the context of this week's lesson, what you sow in others so shall you reap in yourself.

For instance, if you sow hatred, jealousy, and anger, you'll likely get back a lot of resentment. However, if you're generous and give willingly without expecting anything in return, that's what you could get back.

Give encouragement even if you don't feel supportive. Give enthusiasm even if you don't feel enthusiastic. Give a boost of confidence even when you feel doubt.

The principle is pretty simple: You can't give what you don't have. In other words, to give to others you've got to have some of the same quality or emotion. For instance, the act of giving encouragement will grow yours. And in turn, enhanced by your encouragement people will be happy to offer you some of their own. It's that pay-it-forward notion of random acts of kindness.

Sowing what you want to reap is a wonderful way for good feelings and motivational emotions to elevate people. So every day this week, pick at least one person in your life you can encourage. Giving them a compliment on their efforts and telling them to keep up the good work might make their day. It may have been a long time since anyone praised them, and they might be wondering if anyone even notices how hard they're working. Make sure your encouragement is sincere, as insincere flattery falls on deaf ears.

What you'll find amazing is the encouragement you'll get back will make you feel better. Such a simple concept packed with oh-so-many rewards.

Remember: You reap what you sow ... so what will you be sowing this week?

Exercise 13: Inspire Yourself by Inspiring Others

Identify someone who's interested in accomplishing the same goal you're pursuing, but doesn't seem to want to go as far to get it. This could be a friend who is badly out of shape, a writer who just joined the forum you frequent, a student who just joined your dance class, or a guy you met at the last techie Meet Up session who doesn't know how to get started.

Offer to mentor them formally or informally. You might think that working out with someone who isn't in good shape will slow you down. But a weekly session will help you see how far you've come and boost your spirits. It will also help you see yourself as accomplished, knowledgeable, and experienced which can help raise your confidence level. (Plus, it'll force you to exercise ... a win/win!)

If you can't find someone to mentor in person, share your knowledge in online forums. However you choose to do it, give back to someone who's behind you on the learning curve, and enjoy the satisfaction you'll get from helping them.

Remember:

- You're a champion every day and in every way. You know it and every one around you knows it.

- Today, nothing can stand in your way.

- When you need extra determination, you've got it!

- When you need more energy and drive, you've got it!

- You've got the power to get anything done and the patience to overcome challenges, no matter what they may be.

- You can do this and you know you can!

MONDAY
NUMBER 14

The villain that stands between failure and success is **procrastination**. Even my friend, David Herdlinger, calls this pernicious evil 'The biggest country in the world: Procrasti-Nation."

Procrastination – the act of putting off or delaying something requiring immediate attention – can be deadly to your goals and ambitions. Telling yourself "I can do this tomorrow" can become a self-fulfilling prophecy.

There's a joke that says "Don't do today what you can put off for tomorrow." You may have procrastinated in college when you had papers due, and it may have even been a strategy that worked. But you shouldn't give in to procrastination as a matter of habit. One choice to put things off will lead to another, which leads to another, which leads to another. And before you know it, you're in a nursing home wishing you had more time to pursue your dreams (and you still might, but you've gotten into the habit of procrastinating!)

Procrastination – a result of mostly unfounded fears – can cause you great misery, which is no way to live. You need to nip it in the bud by facing your fears, and sacrificing the present in exchange for not having to procrastinate in the future. It's a simple but often difficult formula to follow.

But it doesn't have to be that difficult, as there are ways to beat procrastination that will help you gain greater control over your self-discipline. The first thing you need to do is to break something you've been putting off into a bunch of smaller tasks, and give yourself a reward for completing each one. Even if you spend just one minute on each task, it's still better than putting them off for another day.

The key is to not just break something into smaller components, but to also **get started** at nearly any cost. If it means typing one word to start your novel, do it! Then keep the momentum up with two words, then four words, until you're at a pace that keeps you going full speed ahead.

Exercise 14: Make a Check List

This week you're to focus on breaking big tasks into smaller, more manageable pieces to prevent you from procrastinating. Then tackle at least one to get that monkey off your back and check it off your list. If it seems too daunting, break it into even smaller parts and reward yourself for your extra effort.

At the end of the week schedule any remaining tasks on your calendar so you know they will be completed in a reasonable amount of time. Write them in pen so they can't be erased, and commit to tackling them one at time until they're all checked off and done.

Remember:

- You're a champion every day and in every way. You know it and every one around you knows it.

- Today, nothing can stand in your way.

- When you need extra determination, you've got it!

- When you need more energy and drive, you've got it!

- You've got the power to get anything done and the patience to overcome challenges, no matter what they may be.

- You can do this and you know you can!

MONDAY 15
NUMBER

Can you achieve success by yourself? The short answer is never. The long answer is initiative, leadership, confidence, discipline and courage all come from within. But if you want to build something really big, you eventually have to rely on someone for help. Even novelists who've been cooped up in a cabin for six months have to send their work to a publisher at some point.

You need coaches, cheerleaders, and teammates ... mentors, advisors, consultants ... editors, allies, and positive thinkers. You need anyone who might be willing to contribute to your cause!

This is especially true if you find yourself down in the dumps and frustrated by your lack of success. Think about people as your teammates, cheering you on to win the game. They can support you through tough times, and show you how to find the strength to pick yourself up again. Their belief in you can manifest into self-confidence you never thought you had. If they give you advice, don't be oversensitive. Listen to what they're saying and use it to your benefit.

But what if you don't have encouraging people in your life? What if you try something new, and the people around you offer *dis*couragement instead of *en*couragement? This week you're to focus on what you can do to be the kind of person who attracts more positive people.

Jim Rohn gave the advice that in order to attract attractive people, you must first become attractive.

"But I'm trying to change my life, and no one wants to help!" sounds negative. You need to switch your focus on what you do have, and you'll find that negativity will fly out the window.

Don't be afraid to ask people for help, including your friends and mentors. Most people are happy to be a part of their loved one's dream. And the wisdom, perspective and encouragement they'll give to you will be invaluable.

Exercise 15: Join a Group

This week you're to attend a group activity that supports your efforts to meet your goal, and reinforce that it's possible to achieve success. For example, you might want to go to a...

- Conference

- Trade show

- Local Meet Up

- Group exercise class

- Art show

- Poetry reading, or book reading by a famous author

- Writing group

- Musical group or concert

- Film festival

- Kickstarter event, or opening night of a venture similar

to yours

- Charity benefit

- Mixer

Go with the intention of having a conversation with someone who has either accomplished what you're seeking to achieve, or is pursuing a similar goal. Give them your contact information for follow-up conversations.

Remember:

- You're a champion every day and in every way. You know it and every one around you knows it.

- Today, nothing can stand in your way.

- When you need extra determination, you've got it!

- When you need more energy and drive, you've got it!

- You've got the power to get anything done and the patience to overcome challenges, no matter what they may be.

- You can do this and you know you can!

MONDAY NUMBER 16

Well, it's been four months, which means it's time to give it all up. That's right, give it up!

Now before you get nervous, I don't mean you should give up on the efforts you've been making toward a better life. I mean you should look at any goals you haven't worked on and let go. Chances are this isn't the year for those extra goals you accrued since starting this program. So you're going to put them on the list for next year, or until you've achieved your big goal.

Far be it from me to suggest that anyone should give up on their dreams. But if you're going to focus on one big achievement for the year, you can't have other distractions weighing you down. So it's time to simplify your life by focusing on the one thing that's the most important to you.

You shouldn't feel guilty that you're not working on all the goals on your list, so you need to let go of guilt as well. In fact, let go of everything that can weigh you down, add stress to your life, and ultimately distract you from your most important vision.

You can always go after those goals once you've checked the big one off your list. Did you suddenly get interested in archery? There's no reason you can't eventually take up the sport, but it's not the most important year-end goal on your list, so set it aside.

You're not procrastinating – you're **prioritizing**. During my coaching about goal setting and success, I often like to talk about adding new strategies, tactics, and mindsets to inspire you to greater growth. Sometimes the simplest way is to **prioritize** your goals, and carry forward only the most important one until you attain it.

It's natural that you would have picked up a few other goals over the last four months. Your mind has been energized to think about possibilities. But you're going to set them aside for now. With less on your mind, you'll be able to focus solely on setting your intention to achieve your goal by the end of the year. Then you can reprioritize your goals list to see what you want to tackle next.

Exercise 16: Just Say No

Go through next month's schedule and eliminate all the activities you possibly can. Write apologetic emails and make phone calls to explain that you can't participate for a while, and fill those slots with tasks that will get you closer to your goal.

As for any new commitments or activities, just say no. If that seems too harsh, answer with, "I'll think about it and get back to you." Wait 24 hours before replying, and ask yourself if it will hurt anyone if you decline this one time. You can explain that you had made a commitment that you can't get out of (people are very busy, and they know about committing time to friends and family), but to please keep you in mind for another time.

Remember:

- You're a champion every day and in every way. You know it and every one around you knows it.

- Today, nothing can stand in your way.

- When you need extra determination, you've got it!

- When you need more energy and drive, you've got it!

- You've got the power to get anything done and the patience to overcome challenges, no matter what they may be.

- You can do this and you know you can!

MONDAY
NUMBER **17**

There's an old joke that goes: How do you eat an elephant? Well, one bite at a time of course! If you feel like you're biting off more than you could chew trying to reach your goal, it's time to teach you a number of techniques that will forever change your perspective on this process.

The trick is pretty simple: Let's say you gave your goal a numeric value (i.e., earning $120,000 by the end of 12 months). You'll break it into smaller components until you've arrive at a level you've accomplished before. To make this concept easier:

- Break your goal of $120,000 into 12 months, so now your goal is to earn $10,000 a month. At this point you'll ask yourself, Have I ever earned this much in a month? If you have, skip the next steps. If not, bear with me.

- If you haven't earned $10,000 a month, split it into four weeks which equals $2,500 per week. Have you ever earned $2,500 in a week?

- If not, break that into days: $2500 \div 7 = 500$.

- Have you ever earned $500 in one day? If not, break that into hours. $500 \div 24 = 20.83$.

- Have you ever earned $20.83 in one hour?

See where this is going? Eventually you're going to hit on something that's manageable and an amount you've previously attained.

Once you've arrived at an amount you've made before, you need to look at what you did to earn it. What would it take for you to provide that constant level of productivity to create that small, more manageable amount without feeling like you're overwhelmed?

Once you figure that out, you've arrived at your **new normal** amount you'll need to earn to reach your year-end goal of $120,000. Instead of worrying about the big picture, you've reduced it to less stressful components that are easier to achieve.

This technique isn't limited to income. Maybe you want to lose 48 pounds by the end of the year. Setting a goal of losing two pounds per week can seem much less intimidating, and it'll be fun to check those mini-goals off every seven days.

Giving your goal a numerical value can make it possible to be ambitious without feeling like you've bitten off more than you can chew. Try it this week to see if it doesn't make your efforts seem a little easier, as well as showing you what it would take to perform at that level on a regular basis.

Exercise 17: Measure Your Efforts

You should have your various goal activities on your calendar. For instance, running five miles five times per week should be written down to remind you of your commitment.

Now set a reasonable benchmark – like 30 or 60 days. If you manage to stick to your activities for that period, give yourself a reward. Some examples:

• A manicure or tickets to a game

- A night out with friends

- A new outfit

- A special dinner out

Always choose a reward that's commensurate with the effort, is enjoyable, and gives you an incentive to work even harder.

Remember:

- You're a champion every day and in every way. You know it and every one around you knows it.

- Today, nothing can stand in your way.

- When you need extra determination, you've got it!

- When you need more energy and drive, you've got it!

- You've got the power to get anything done and the patience to overcome challenges, no matter what they may be.

- You can do this and you know you can!

MONDAY 18
NUMBER

What if you set your goal at 50 when you could do 100? For this lesson, what the goal is isn't important. What is important is not to limit your potential because you're setting goals that are too small.

Last week you learned a technique for dealing with biting off more than you can chew. This week you'll be taught how to question whether your goals are difficult to bite into in the first place, and that you're capable of achieving more than you realized.

Consider the story of George Dantzig in Cynthia Kersey's book, Unstoppable. As a college student, George always studied hard. One day he overslept and found himself 20 minutes late for class. He quickly copied two math problems on the board he thought was the homework assignment. After several days of hair pulling and frustration, he finally figured the problems out and put the homework on the professor's desk the next day.

One Sunday morning George was awakened at six a.m. by his excited professor saying that he had solved the problems when no one else could. (Because he was late to class, George hadn't heard his professor announce the equations were brain teasers that even Albert Einstein couldn't figure out. Because George thought it was "just" homework, he had no preconceived idea of his limitations. He accomplished his goal simply because **he didn't know he couldn't!**)

What does this say about self-imposed limitations or self-fulfilling prophecies? Are they more powerful than massive action and hard work? Are people better off assuming they can do great things and progress from there? If you ask me, most people could benefit from a good goal boost by pushing their ambitions into the stratosphere.

You shouldn't wait for self-confidence to come; you should *demand* that it comes so that you can accomplish your goal. Dantzig did just that because *he didn't know he couldn't.*

The good news about all this? The same person who's been setting your limits happens to be the same person it takes to remove them: **You!** So, what can you do this week you didn't know you couldn't?

Exercise 18: A Private Challenge

This week you're going to do something privately that scares you. Some "outrageous feat" that pushes your boundaries. (Next week you'll attempt something publicly that intimidates you, so this is the dress rehearsal for doing something you aren't sure you can do.)

To help you understand this exercise better, you can read next week's exercise to see what you need to prepare for your big challenge. You want this to be scary, exciting, and a bit intimidating. If you aim for something you know you can accomplish, you'll rob yourself of the thrill of victory.

This week you'll choose an intimidating feat that you'll take on next week. After you've chosen it you'll want to:

• Break it into manageable components.

- Analyze each component and decide what needs to be done to accomplish it.

- Make a list, a graph or a chart to visually help you.

- Research examples of others who have gone before you and succeeded.

- Rehearse what you're going to say.

- Visualize yourself attempting the feat and succeeding (i.e., cold-calling a new client and getting the order).

Spend your week dreaming of possibilities and preparing for the big push next week! (Remember, you don't know you can't do this … you just know it's your "homework" and you'll push through until you find an answer.)

Remember:

- You're a champion every day and in every way. You know it and every one around you knows it.

- Today, nothing can stand in your way.

- When you need extra determination, you've got it!

- When you need more energy and drive, you've got it!

- You've got the power to get anything done and the patience to overcome challenges, no matter what they may be.

- You can do this and you know you can!

MONDAY *19*
NUMBER

This week is all about *trailblazing*. (Of course this isn't literal. You can't very well accomplish your goal by macheting your way through thick jungle foliage, unless your actual goal is to be the next Dr. Livingston. However, I'm guessing that isn't the case.)

What kind of trailblazing *am* I talking about? It's about being the "edge of your blade" or "the tip of the spear" in your own success. To help you better understand, put on your pith helmet and let's get into the "thicket" of things.

Let's say you want to approach a member of the opposite sex in a social gathering, but as usual you come up with a thousand excuses like:

- I'm so nervous that I'll probably embarrass myself.

- I just need a little more experience being social. Then I can finally have enough confidence to approach someone.

- I need to go home and do affirmations to buoy my confidence so I can approach people in these situations.

So you leave feeling despondent, unworthy, and angry at yourself for not having the courage or self-confidence to approach someone who might have really enjoyed meeting you.

What do all these excuses have in common? They assume you'll be successful before you make the effort.

I'm here to tell you that you can't get emotionally strong unless you step outside your comfort zone. You can't acquire self-confidence *before* you take action; you only gain self-confidence *as a result of having taken action.*

Let me repeat that: **You only gain self-confidence as a result of having taken action.**

In essence you need to drag your confidence, competence, and your skill sets with you as you charge into the world. *You* have to be the tip of the spear or the edge of the blade hacking your way through the thickets of life. Sure this can be painful. You'll probably encounter a few thorns as you trailblaze into unknown territory.

Maybe you approach a member of the opposite sex and it goes badly, but that short-term pain is what will give you the long-term success. You'll gain the confidence you need to approach *after* you approach and not before. In many ways it'll feel like you're bluffing through life, but at some point everyone bluffs their way up the ladder.

If you've never had a client pay you $10,000 before, there has to be a first time. So you make the sale, *then* let the confidence come. You blaze the trail by poking your subconscious with the tip of a spear or hacking down obstacles with your machete. You can develop the traits you desire by taking action so bold that it *has* to give you those qualities in order to thrive. Then your subconscious figures that if you're going to keep taking these actions it had better help you out.

Be the tip of the spear, be the machete. Do some scary things this week, and watch how increased confidence comes *after* risk.

Exercise 19: Attempt Something that Seems Unattainable

Choose one outrageous feat to attempt this week and give it your all. For example, you could:

- Cold call a potential client and ask for a fee 50% higher than you've ever charged before.

- Offer a service you've never provided before, but want to have on your portfolio.

- Exercise 25% longer than you've ever exercised before.

- Submit your work to a prominent newspaper, journal, or art show.

- Go out to a singles mixer and approach the most attractive person in the room.

- Record a new song, write a poem or a short story in an intimidating, new format.

- Fast for a day.

- Ask your boss for a promotion.

- Apply for a new job.

- Submit an application to a venture capitalist.

- Apply for a grant.

- Put up a new website.

Daring yourself to reach something unattainable is the only way to overcome the doubts holding you back.

Remember:

- You're a champion every day and in every way. You know it and every one around you knows it.

- Today, nothing can stand in your way.

- When you need extra determination, you've got it!

- When you need more energy and drive, you've got it!

- You've got the power to get anything done and the patience to overcome challenges, no matter what they may be.

- You can do this and you know you can!

MONDAY
NUMBER 20

You're approaching the halfway point of the year. If you look back at all the steps you've taken towards success, what would your tracks look like? Would they lead straight to your current position? Or would they zigzag everywhere and not make any sense?

In geometry the shortest path between two points is a straight line, or "as the crow flies." As it applies to this week's lesson, the straighter your path the closer you've come to your goal.

"True north" is the direction along the earth's surface towards the geographic North Pole. When applied to goal setting, it refers to how accurately you're pointed and moving toward achieving your goal. If you look objectively at where you're at, would it be a step toward your true north or a step back?

How do you find *your* true north? How do you zero in on that for the rest of the year to prevent wasting as little time as possible?

Simple: **You need to focus**. Focus is one of the more underrated aspects of achievement because people don't understand its power. The focus of a magnifying glass makes the sun's rays capable of burning through paper. Focus is what allows concentrated streams of water to cut through metal, or lasers to cut through pretty much anything. Without focus your goals can beat you. But *with focus you are unbeatable.*

Let's face it, much of the time life gets in the way. Remember earlier when I mentioned John Lennon's saying, "Life is what happens to you while you're busy making other plans"? Boy, does that apply to goal setting more than ever!

To help you maintain focus on a long term basis, you're going to create new habits. Be aware of all the steps you're taking, especially when you're taking action. Ask yourself if the steps are really helping you to achieve your goals, or if they're wasting your time.

For example, maybe you're writing a novel. Which action will galvanize you into action? Reading a blog about writing a novel, or writing your first chapter of the actual novel? Focusing on what you truly want will change all your priorities.

Exercise 20: Add Another Daily Habit

It's time to add another habit to the first one you established at the beginning of the year to remind you of your goal every single day. Take your time to choose a habit that's simple and doable. Then repeat the exercises at the beginning of the program including:

- Telling someone else, or reporting about your new habit to your accountability system.

- Schedule your habit on the calendar each day.

- Post sticky-notes everywhere to remind you about your new habit.

- Mark it off each day when you've accomplished your habit.

This daily habit should keep you focused on your goal, even if all you do is look yourself in the mirror each morning and say, "I **will** reach my goal by the end of the year."

Remember:

- You're a champion every day and in every way. You know it and every one around you knows it.

- Today, nothing can stand in your way.

- When you need extra determination, you've got it!

- When you need more energy and drive, you've got it!

- You've got the power to get anything done and the patience to overcome challenges, no matter what they may be.

- You can do this and you know you can!

MONDAY
NUMBER 21

Wayne Gretzky once said, "You miss 100% of the shots you don't take." That's a terrific nugget of wisdom from hockey's greatest player and all-time leading scorer.

Think of it this way: Maybe you like to hike. You know that tripping on a rock and skinning your knee is a possibility, but you brave it anyway and have a good time. But what if the risk rose to 98%? Would you still do it if you really loved to hike? Of course you would, because you'd know that the 2% is worth the effort. If you trip and fall, you'd get back up, dust yourself off and continue the hike. Your chances of tripping if you don't go hiking? Zero percent. You're perfectly safe. But you don't get to the top of the hill and see the beautiful expanse of God's country.

People who expect to score 100% of the time are dismayed when not all their shots go into the basket, not all their leads will buy from them, or not all of their blog readers will subscribe to their newsletter. So what? If you accomplish one thing more than you would have while lying on the couch, you're moving in the right direction.

Would you rather have a 1% chance at getting a better paying job, or a 0% chance?

Would you rather have a 50% chance of making the sale, or a 0% chance? The odds tilt in your favor the longer you persist.

You're bound to succeed – it's just a matter of mathematical probabilities.

Wouldn't it be great if people realized that's how easy success could be if they just gave it time and kept going? This week you're going to learn how your odds can improve when you make it part of your habit to take action.

Exercise 21: Add Action to Your New Habit

Find a small action to connect to your new daily habit. It should be small and simple; something that can propel you towards your goal. Let's say you decided to announce your goal to yourself in the mirror each morning. If your goal is to lose 20 pounds this year, you could add 30 squats or 50 sit-ups to your daily affirmation. Then record your action as part of your daily habit on your calendar, accountability mechanism, and your planner.

Remember:

- You're a champion every day and in every way. You know it and every one around you knows it.

- Today, nothing can stand in your way.

- When you need extra determination, you've got it!

- When you need more energy and drive, you've got it!

- You've got the power to get anything done and the patience to overcome challenges, no matter what they may be.

- You can do this and you know you can!

MONDAY
NUMBER 22

This week is all about keeping track of your progress. How far are you into your journey, and how close are you to achieving your goal?

In this case, honesty is the best policy. Even if you don't have an exact number figure as to where you are at this point, you should try to estimate it as close as possible.

Keeping track isn't about where your progress is or isn't. It should be an indication as to whether or not you need to experiment with different strategies to break through a plateau. If your goal is to put aside $10,000 in savings and you've only saved $1,900, now is the time to ramp up your efforts by trying something new, or brainstorming ways you can change your strategy.

People get so caught up in the day-to-day efforts of reaching their goals that they neglect to keep track of their progress. In many cases they haven't put forth the effort because they're afraid that when they look at the scoreboard the results will be depressing. They've found that keeping track of their progress can be a delicate balance. On one hand, seeing their successes can be inspiring. On the other hand, realizing they've plateaued can be discouraging.

I hate to tell you this, but your success requires that you keep track of your progress. Without this barometer you'll never know when to change your strategies.

How do I personally measure my progress? This may come as a surprise to some people, but the only thing I have control over is my efforts. The results usually involve factors outside myself, while my effort is totally from within.

In 1980 the U.S. boycotted the Olympic Games. Had I been an athlete training to win a gold medal, I might have measured my progress by the end result and would have been terribly disappointed. However, if I measured my progress by how much training made me into a better athlete, I would have been pleased with the results. What happened at the Games was beyond my control, but I got my "gold medal" through the expensive, rigorous training I received.

You need to make your progress tracking as objective as possible. You want to know when what you're doing is working, and when it might be time to try something new.

This week you're going to take time to accurately review your progress to find out what the real score is. Then you'll know if you're winning. Or of it's time for a second half comeback that will still win the game, even if it's not in the way you first envisioned it.

Exercise 22: Numbers Count

Come up with a numerical assessment of your progress on your plan thus far, and how much further you have to go.

Then come up with a measurable plan to accomplish your goal by the end of the year. Research plans other people have used to accomplish similar goals. Compare them to your own and see if you're on track.

Then look for ideas to speed your progress and to sustain you as you pursue your goal. Record your findings in a journal, on your calendar, or within your accountability system.

Remember:

- You're a champion every day and in every way. You know it and every one around you knows it.

- Today, nothing can stand in your way.

- When you need extra determination, you've got it!

- When you need more energy and drive, you've got it!

- You've got the power to get anything done and the patience to overcome challenges, no matter what they may be.

- You can do this and you know you can!

MONDAY

Some people think King Solomon was the wisest man who ever lived. In the Book of Ecclesiastes he says in essence that two people are better than one, because if one falls the other can help him up. Such a simple, noble concept. Yet, how many people ignore this maxim because they want to accomplish everything on their own, or are afraid to ask for help?

This week's lesson is two people earn more money together than they could on their own, because they help balance each other's strengths and weaknesses.

What does this have to do with year-end goal? If, for example, your goal is fitness, there isn't much "profit" in having a workout partner or a personal trainer. You don't burn more calories just because someone is working out with you.

But without someone standing by your side to correct your weightlifting form, you'll never know what you're doing wrong and you can ruin your back. Therefore, just about any personal goal can benefit from having someone help it along the way.

Are you delegating tasks that need to be completed to achieve your year-end goal? How could you spend your time better? Could you enlist the help of others in order to achieve your goal? Remember, people who work with you are on your team. They're going to help you achieve your goal, even if their feedback isn't always a pleasant pill to swallow.

This week you're to take a look at all the action steps you have left. You're going to carefully analyze each of them, and figure out which ones should be delegated. Time is a valuable commodity, and you have to decide where it's better spent.

Here are some times when it's correct to delegate to others:

- When the work is tedious and laborious (i.e., data entry).

- When the work can be done better (i.e., a consultant).

- When someone can offer an objective eye (i.e., a personal trainer, or someone to edit your novel).

- When the work involves skills you don't have or don't perform well

This week you're going to focus on delegating work others can do for you.

Exercise 23: Find A Buddy

Find someone – if you haven't already – who can be an accountability partner for the remainder of the year. It can be someone from a social group, someone you look up to, or someone you've inspired. Whoever this person is, ask them to commit to your goal until the end of the year.

Meet with them this week to discuss how you can pursue your goal together. Devise a plan for when one or both of you loses motivation or fails to meet a goal. Come up with ways to inspire each other and to maintain motivation you're both comfortable with.

Remember:

- You're a champion every day and in every way. You know it and every one around you knows it.

- Today, nothing can stand in your way.

- When you need extra determination, you've got it!

- When you need more energy and drive, you've got it!

- You've got the power to get anything done and the patience to overcome challenges, no matter what they may be.

- You can do this and you know you can!

MONDAY

One of my favorite success stories comes from an extraordinary event I had the privilege of witnessing first-hand. On April 12, 1981, I watched the very first space shuttle – the STS-1 – launch from a vantage point as close as any civilians were allowed at the Kennedy Space Center north of Cape Canaveral.

During all the excitement and noise, I was thinking about how long the shuttle seemed to hover on the pad before it actually began to rise. As I found out later, it took more than 80% of the fuel to get the shuttle up the first mile; the other 20% got the shuttle through the rest of its journey. What an astounding metaphor for success and momentum!

Consider that when you want to construct something big – like a skyscraper – you have to spend most of the time and effort on building the foundation. Building towards success can take a lot of time and energy before you start seeing the fruits of your labor.

But if you continue burning fuel, if you keep digging a foundation, you're positioning yourself to build something really spectacular. Once you break through your "momentum barrier," you'll find you only need about 20% more fuel to keep going.

I learned that same principle when I used to jog in the morning. I didn't stop when I got too tired or winded; I slowed down just enough to get my breath back. And once it came back, I could jog faster because I never lost my momentum. I learned that it's easier to start from a slower pace than it is to start jogging while walking or standing still.

Before you completely stop the efforts you've been making because you've yet to see results, consider what it would do to your momentum. Working just **one minute a day** on your year-end goal won't break the chain of action. You'll find it will become much easier to eventually work **one hour a day** on your goal since you had never quit your momentum.

Exercise 24: Make Every Minute Count

This week you're to commit to a specific number of minutes you'll work on your goal. Tell your accountability partner what your plan is and report in each day (or after a certain period of time) to tell them how things are going.

Every moment should be spent in intense, meaningful movement forward towards your goal. Make them count! Run harder, swim harder, or write in focused spurts. Don't become distracted by surfing the Web, listening to music or playing online games.

Have coffee with someone new if your goal is to find a romantic relationship, and really put yourself out there while you talk. Or shut yourself off from the world for those few moments and make them count towards your goal, whatever that may be.

Remember:

- You're a champion every day and in every way. You know it and every one around you knows it.

- Today, nothing can stand in your way.

- When you need extra determination, you've got it!

- When you need more energy and drive, you've got it!

- You've got the power to get anything done and the patience to overcome challenges, no matter what they may be

- You can do this and you know you can!

MONDAY

Last week's lesson mentioned the necessity of maintaining your momentum. This week I'll go into even greater detail about this the notion of **persistence**. Persistence can be the single-most important thing that will drive your efforts to success.

The law of success boils down to one important piece of advice you'll hear from anyone who's ever accomplished something great: **Don't give up!** But is success really as simple as not giving up? Of course it isn't, because there are many other factors involved. And yes, life *is* an art. It's complex and multi-layered, and the methods people use to mold reality for their purposes are also complex.

Last week I talked about never giving up, even if it meant spending only one minute a day on your goal. It would be better for you to get dressed in gym clothes, drive down to the gym, and do only one step on a treadmill if the alternative was to not go at all.

Why is this so important? No matter what other elements are present in your journey, how hard you're trying, how much time you spend per day on your goal, none of that means anything if you give up.

Persistence! The greatest tool you'll gain during your 52-week journey to success. You see, magical things can happen when you persist every day, even in the most minute amounts. But you won't know unless you keep going.

So this week you're to focus on how you can persist. I'm not advocating that you go to the gym for only five minutes – of course you can do better than that. But if that's all you can muster, that's all that's in your heart at the moment, then you drag yourself there in order to keep your habit alive. One minute leads to five to ten … and eventually you'll have committed a good amount of time to an entire routine.

Habit … action … persistence … outcome … success!

Exercise 25: Talk to Someone You Admire

Contact someone you admire who has made great strides in your field of interest. Ask for an interview, email questions about how they achieved their success, or invite them out for coffee.

Or you can go online and start researching for a fabulous blogger, author, life coach or motivational speaker (whoever it is you're targeting) who will respond to your query and give you inspirational words of wisdom. Nothing ventured, nothing gained!

Remember:

- You're a champion every day and in every way. You know it and every one around you knows it.

- Today, nothing can stand in your way.

- When you need extra determination, you've got it!

- When you need more energy and drive, you've got it!

- You've got the power to get anything done and the patience to overcome challenges, no matter what they may be.

- You can do this and you know you can!

MONDAY 26
NUMBER

There's a bit of magic in what I'm going to share with you this week. Sure, it may be one of the oldest tricks in the book. But I use the word "trick" loosely since it's is a solid, time-proven technique for achieving goals.

Ready? Here goes:

Act as if. Let me repeat that: **Act … as … if.**

Let's say you want to be debt free. How would you act if you were debt free? Would you feel better about spending money? Would you think about the things you could do if you didn't have to worry about money?

You might argue that acting as if you had no debt is what got you into your financial mess in the first place. But consider this: If you act like a debt-free person, you'll have to take the same actions a debt-free person would take to *stay* debt-free.

It was Aristotle who said "to do is to be." You can't be something before you take on the habits of that something. For instance, if you want to be fit, you can't expect to be fit before going to the gym; it's only through doing the exercises that your body conforms to your actions. *Being* fit is a result of your actions.

That's why you have to set the standard right now for what you want to be and start acting that way. You have to *do* the things that will force your body and mind to conform to what you want to *be*. **To do is to be.**

You have to "drag" yourself to the progress you want. Ask yourself how you would act if you achieve your goal (a more positive affirmation would be "when"). If you get that promotion at work, how would you dress to fit the part? Then you'll start dressing that way even before you get the promotion. Would you have to work harder to remain accountable for your higher salary? Work as if you've already reached that level.

If you see where this is going, you'll understand how strong the principle **act as if** is and how much it can change your life.

Exercise 26: Label Yourself a Success

What label will you use when you've reached your success? Singer? Runner? Husband? Wife? Parent? Homeowner? Artist? Entrepreneur? Freelancer? Consultant? Small business owner?

Start referring to yourself in present tense with this label, even in public (if socially appropriate). Invest in paraphernalia with this label on it (for example, you might buy a t-shirt that says "Runner Girl," or a coffee mug that says "World's Best Boss"). If nothing else, address yourself as if you've already succeeded while you work toward your goals.

Remember:

- You're a champion every day and in every way. You know it and every one around you knows it.

- Today, nothing can stand in your way.

- When you need extra determination, you've got it!

- When you need more energy and drive, you've got it!

- You've got the power to get anything done and the patience to overcome challenges, no matter what they may be.

- You can do this and you know you can!

MONDAY
NUMBER 27

Last week I discussed the principle of "acting as if": Before you can **be** something, you have to **do** the actions that result in the being. In other words, the *doing* will always come before the *being*.

This means you're going to have to accelerate your self-expectations. If you had trouble imagining yourself in the role of your dreams last week, you need to find ways to expand your concept of what things could be like when you achieve your goal.

There will be a lot of positive benefits associated with achieving success. Isn't that why you're trying to achieve the goal in the first place? You want to get yourself from where you are now to a place of abundance and security, and there's absolutely nothing wrong with that. It really shouldn't be hard to envision yourself living well, daring greatly, and being successful.

But people don't often talk about the negatives of achieving success. The honest truth is if you want to achieve success, you're going to have to live with those as well. Of course the positives should far outweigh the negatives. But if you want to assure a role in your new life after you've achieved your goal, you have to know what the negatives are and prepare yourself to handle them.

Many people who have lost a lot of weight say they have trouble picturing themselves as thin and attractive, even when everyone is telling them how good they look. They also grow cynical when they see how much better people are treating them.

A promotion at work might mean a raise and congratulations from your friends and family, but will it bring additional responsibility?

Examples like this wouldn't normally be obstacles to success. But if you want to "do" the actions to "be" successful, you're going to have to be aware of these kinds of things. Preparing yourself to confront the hard stuff that comes with success will help you do an even better job at imagining yourself in your new role.

Exercise 27: Prepare for the Reality of Success

This week you're to find someone who has succeeded in accomplishing the same goal, and ask them about the positive and negative aspects of success. For example, you could talk to a successful artist about their struggles to fill all the orders for their sculptures.

Or you could ask a successful internet marketing guru about their struggles to keep up with their clients, and if they've had to hire subcontractors.

You could talk to a successful bakery owner about paying overhead costs, and getting up at atrocious hours to keep the showcase full of baked goods.

Take notes while you speak to this person, then plan how you'll handle meeting your goal. Let the good and bad of success permeate your days as you daydream about your new role, which will make it more plausible and real.

Remember:

- You're a champion every day and in every way. You know it and every one around you knows it.

- Today, nothing can stand in your way.

- When you need extra determination, you've got it!

- When you need more energy and drive, you've got it!

- You've got the power to get anything done and the patience to overcome challenges, no matter what they may be.

- You can do this and you know you can!

MONDAY
NUMBER 28

Congratulations! If you've gotten to this point you've persisted a lot longer than most people. While you've been struggling and pushing your way to success in a way you never have before, you may not have realized that you're over the halfway point. Well, maybe you noticed it and maybe you didn't. Maybe it feels like halfway. Maybe it feels like you should be three-fourths of the way by now.

Instead of focusing on what's happened already, let's focus on a concept that people who follow American sports can relate to: Halftime. In both basketball and football halftime is an integral part of the game. It's a time to regroup, reassess strategy, and to rest before the next half of the game begins.

If you've made it this far but your results aren't where you want them to be, don't worry. The first half has ended but the game is far from over. Even professional athletes often have to struggle in the second half of a game in order to come back from a deficit and eventually squeeze out a victory. Almost every case of a comeback is due to a change in strategy at halftime. Many times it's a team focusing on the basics of executing the game plan.

So what's your lesson this week? No matter how great or poor your first half was, the second half is more critical. And you can make it whatever you wish it to be.

If your first half wasn't up to your expectations, you can take the lessons you and change your strategy to supercharge your success. If your first half was more successful than you ever dreamed, now is the time to remember that only one-half of the year has passed, and if you quit now your dream can be lost. Now isn't the time to become complacent (complacency should be eliminated from your vocabulary!).

Wins or losses aren't given based on half of a game; they're given to the team still standing when the final buzzer goes off.

This week's lesson is for you to think about what you're going to do in the second half of your game. What strategies do you need to rethink? Where do you need to keep plugging away?

Exercise 28: Go Out on a Limb

This is where you'll review your progress these past 27 weeks. Which habits did you establish, and which never took root? What efforts paid off, and which ones flopped?

This week you're going to do something risky. You might…

- Go for a long ride with a cycling group, knowing you'll probably be the slowest biker.

- Ask an English professor to critique what you've written so far in your novel, or poetry anthology.

- Ask for an informational interview for a position you want.

- Go on a college tour, then sign up to see if you can get accepted into a program.

- Talk to your Human Resources department about possible openings at your workplace that are more appealing.

- Ask your accountability partner for a challenge and accept it, even if it feels unreasonable.

- Get a trusted friend to look over your wardrobe and help you dress for dating success.

Taking action can make yourself vulnerable, but you also set yourself up for success. If you don't get the answers you were hoping for, learn from your efforts. And promise yourself you'll take action to advance to a place where you'll succeed in the future.

Remember:

- You're a champion every day and in every way. You know it and every one around you knows it.

- Today, nothing can stand in your way.

- When you need extra determination, you've got it!

- When you need more energy and drive, you've got it!

- You've got the power to get anything done and the patience to overcome challenges, no matter what they may be

- You can do this and you know you can!

MONDAY
NUMBER 29

This week I'm going to begin with a story.

Plato, a student of Socrates the great Greek philosopher, asked him how he could gain wisdom. Socrates told Plato to walk with him to the edge of the ocean. They walked into the water up to the point where it was about four feet deep (enough to cover most men at that time). At this point Socrates grabbed Plato, plunged his head under the water and held him there. Plato became frantic and struggled desperately to get free, but Socrates wouldn't let him up.

At the very last minute Socrates lifted him out of the water. After Plato regained consciousness he accused Socrates of trying to drown him. Socrates said, "If that would have been my intention, I wouldn't have pulled you ashore. When you desire my knowledge like you desired that breath of air, then you shall have it."

It's such a simple – albeit somewhat macabre – lesson. But the power lies within its simplicity: **With enough desire, *nothing will stop you*.**

The question is, then, how do you achieve desire? You first start with a simple desire: your goal. Just about everyone has this amount of desire – it's really not a big deal.

However, if you take action toward a goal, you'll have a greater desire that actually **motivates** you (puts you into motion). But working hard one day and then quitting doesn't mean you have desire; it just means you were motivated one day and that was that.

So where does a great deal of desire come from? It comes from a near-obsessive level of thinking about your goals and putting action toward them; of taking the energy you spend in a day and focusing on what you want.

The Law of Intention states "Whatever you put your attention on increases. Whatever you remove your attention from disintegrates and disappears." How often do you daydream about other things while working on a goal you're only half-heartedly interested in? How can you start putting those daydreams to use?

Exercise 29: Visualize Success

Dig out your goals journal and write out the story about when you meet your goal from start to finish. Including challenges you've overcome, and the person you've changed into once you succeed.

Read your success story each night before you go to bed. Linger on the most exciting and appealing parts, such as how it will feel to finally succeed or how you think other people will respond to your success. After you turn out the lights daydream about your success, and repeat the story over and over until you fall asleep.

Remember:

- You're a champion every day and in every way. You know it and every one around you knows it.

- Today, nothing can stand in your way.

- When you need extra determination, you've got it!

- When you need more energy and drive, you've got it!

- You've got the power to get anything done and the patience to overcome challenges, no matter what they may be

- You can do this and you know you can!

MONDAY NUMBER 30

What if you've quit by this point? (You must still be considering continuing, or you wouldn't be reading this page.) Quitting one's goals can be very discouraging. You feel that not only have you wasted time, but that you've wasted another year of your life. Then without thinking, you ascribe your dreams to the beginning of next year and give up on the rest of your 52 weeks.

Take "there's always next year" out of your vocabulary, because this week you're going to start again if you've quit or feel like quitting.

A lot of people let time they've lost nag at them. They fret about what they could have accomplished if they'd begun a year earlier. Or where they could have been if they'd stuck with a particular goal (which, sadly, is another form of procrastination). It's almost as if they're putting off things by dwelling on the past. Then they say they'll start again tomorrow, next week, next month, or next year.

Well, dear friend, that's **not** going to be you. Not this time. But you have to be willing to start on your new life today.

Yes, today!

You see, many people have a fairytale ideal about their future selves. They think that one day they'll magically decide to change their lives, and magically will have all the motivation they need. They don't do it today because they think it's not easy to become that kind of person, so they wait until someone hands them a magic wand and *poof!* All their problems are solved.

So they put it off and "today" becomes "One day I'll..." Eventually, tomorrow *will* come, and it will feel just like today because nothing will have happened. It won't get any easier, and you're not going to get any younger. Today is as young as you'll ever be. Today is the earliest possible starting point you have.

Consider this quote by the explorer W. H. Murray: "There is one elementary truth the ignorance of which kills countless ideas and splendid plans: that the moment one definitely commits oneself, then Providence moves too.

All sorts of things occur to help one that would never otherwise have occurred. A whole stream of events issues from the decision, raising in one's favor all manner of unforeseen incidents and meetings and material assistance which no man could have dreamed would have come his way. Whatever you can do or dream you can begin it. Boldness has genius, power and magic in it."

Better words have seldom been spoken!

Exercise 30: Restart the Clock!

This is the week you'll reassess your progress and your goals, restart if you've fallen off the wagon, and think of it as a new venture even if you've been plugging along all year long. You can...

- Step on the scale.

- Measure how many push-ups you can do or how far you can run.

- Check your bank account.

- Update your resume.

- Go through your contacts list.

Once you get a sober estimate of where you're at and where you want to go, you'll set a daily habit in place that will get you one baby step closer to your goal.

Maybe you'll smile at every person you meet, or you'll do 30 jumping jacks each morning before getting in the shower. Maybe you'll log on to that business support forum each day and read what other entrepreneurs are doing. Whatever it is, it's got to be simple and positive, and something you can do every single day.

Now contact your accountability partner and state what your habit is going to be. Recommit to your goal. Ask for their help to remain focused and motivated. Reset the clock this week as if it's the first time you've decided to pursue your goal.

Remember:

- You're a champion every day and in every way. You know it and every one around you knows it.

- Today, nothing can stand in your way.

- When you need extra determination, you've got it!

- When you need more energy and drive, you've got it!

- You've got the power to get anything done and the patience to overcome challenges, no matter what they may be

- You can do this and you know you can!

MONDAY
NUMBER **31**

Dreams don't die loudly ... they die slowly and quietly. They die when you put off that last repetition at the gym until next week. They die when you let cynicism sweep over your heart as opposed to correcting attitude and choosing a better future.

No one warns you when your dreams are fading. You only realize it when they're not present, and sometimes not even until much later when the negatives of the world have overtaken your thinking and you've become dispirited.

Dispiritedness and disappointment are the **real** perils of life. Many people believe that obstacles, failure, ridicule, embarrassment, and mistakes are things to fear.

The only thing you need to fear are thoughts such as, "I shouldn't take action because I don't want to risk ridicule." "I don't want to risk making a mistake." "I don't want to be disappointed again." The real defeat occurs as thoughts you give yourself.

You see, there's no battle as tough or taxing as the battle you wage inside your mind. You're your own worst critic, and you're the one who determines how you see the world.

Of course obstacles exist. But they're less important than your attitude toward them, or the decision you make internally as to how to treat those obstacles.

Will your fears be your barriers? Or will they be opportunities for growth? It's time to focus on the relationship with yourself, and don't let disappointment and dispiritedness take root in your heart. You need to win the battle against negative emotions and come out on top. Whatever happens on the outside is nothing compared to the strength you can find on the inside.

Exercise 31: The Mood Barometer

This week you need to ask yourself at least three times a day "How do I feel about my goal?" If at any point you feel discouraged or guilty, do something that's been physiologically proven to improve despondency. Some quick fixes for the blues are:

- Go for a 20-minute walk or jog.

- Get outside in the sun.

- Sit under a happy light (ultraviolet light) for 15 minutes.

- Listen to upbeat music.

- Eat a piece of chocolate or drink a cup of coffee.

- Talk to a friend who makes you feel better.

- Watch a funny video or read funny comics.

- Dance as if your life depends on it.

- Do jumping jacks

All these actions are scientifically proven to help jar you out of a bad mood and to revitalize you. Be sure to take action immediately, and refuse to allow yourself to wallow in discouragement or guilt.

Remember:

- You're a champion every day and in every way. You know it and every one around you knows it.

- Today, nothing can stand in your way.

- When you need extra determination, you've got it!

- When you need more energy and drive, you've got it!

- You've got the power to get anything done and the patience to overcome challenges, no matter what they may be

- You can do this and you know you can!

MONDAY
NUMBER 32

Charlie "Tremendous" Jones had a great saying: "You are the same today as you'll be in five years, except for two things: the books you read and the people you meet and associate with." That's quite a reasonable recipe for success, especially if you want to change yourself over the next five years.

So this begs the question, how much time do you spend each day reading a personal development book? Or a biography of someone you admire?

Creating the habit of reading even just 15 minutes every day can radically alter your life. The changes won't necessarily manifest on a day-to-day basis. But over a period of five years your attitudes will shift, and your view of the world will be totally different.

The people you know also affect who you'll become. Many scientists believe that even something like obesity is "socially contagious" in that it's not actually spread virally, but through the phenomenon of social psychology. So if being around overweight people can contribute to you becoming obese, it should follow that being around positive people can make you positive and so on.

The next habit you'll want to develop is to find people you can learn from. Chances are the people you hang out with now aren't stretching your thinking enough. You don't have to give up their friendship, but adding people who have big dreams and ambitions, especially if they're much bigger than yours, to your life will have a profound effect on your perspective. You'll be amazed at just how quickly these new habits and acquaintances can rewire your thinking in just a few weeks, let alone five years.

Exercise 32: Read to Grow

Choose a book on self-development, strategy, or someone's biography. Read it for 15 minutes each night before you go to bed, or first thing each morning if you're an early riser. Jot down whatever stuck with you or inspired you towards your goal.

Remember:

- You're a champion every day and in every way. You know it and every one around you knows it.

- Today, nothing can stand in your way.

- When you need extra determination, you've got it!

- When you need more energy and drive, you've got it!

- You've got the power to get anything done and the patience to overcome challenges, no matter what they may be

- You can do this and you know you can!

MONDAY 33
NUMBER

Sometimes you desire a goal, but you don't seem to be in perfect harmony with it. This, of course, can create a lot of resistance on your road to success.

You might be pushing when you should be pulled. You might be pushing when you want to be doing something else. And at the end of the night you drift to sleep thinking about what else you could be doing with your time.

That's no way to pursue a goal, and I know it from firsthand experience. For many years I tried to set health goals, but was never in harmony with them. For whatever reason, it never really mattered whether or not I achieved them. As far as I was concerned, they were other people's goals they wanted for me. Even though I took action, my negative attitude eventually won out. The end result? I constantly chastised myself for not being able to achieve those goals.

Chances are you've been in that same boat at some point in your life. So how do you break out of your resistance?

You need to reexamine the reasons for your goal, and determine steps you can take to create a "white-hot" desire for it. You need to create an action that exceeds the action you think you need to take. Eventually you'll break through your resistance, and enter a state of harmony with the attitude you've been looking for all along.

In order to be in harmony with your goal you need to find which belief is limiting you and erase it immediately. Soon your new beliefs will pull you toward your goal rather than having to constantly fight uphill.

As any kid sitting in a little red wagon will tell you, it's much more fun to be pulled than to push. And it's much more fun to be going downhill than uphill!

Exercise 33: Find an Enjoyable Way to Achieve Your Goal

Talk to your accountability partner or people in your online forum about what parts of the process they've enjoyed thus far. Then start a new page in your journal. Draw a line down the middle of the page and label one side "Hate" and the other side "Love."

On the "hate" side list parts of this process you despise. On the "love" side list of parts you love. (Don't worry about the parts that are just "okay.")

The next step is to see if you can eliminate one "hate" from your list, and increase the time you spend on the "love" side of your goal plan. Ask yourself if there are more things you "love" that you could add into your plan. Use the following examples as inspiration while you figure out what this means for you:

- Maybe you're trying to meet a romantic partner. You hate the bar scene but have enjoyed meeting people at classes, so you can look into classes filled primarily with people of the right gender.

- Maybe you're trying to start a new business. You love working on the website and product development end of things, but hate marketing. Look into hiring a marketing guru part time to take over that piece of the effort.

- Maybe you're trying to lose weight. You hate how overheated and sweaty you get when you run, so look into swimming or exercising in a gym.

- Maybe you're working two jobs while you start a side business. Look into hiring someone to do your lawn work or to clean your house once a month.

In other words, find a way to make the pursuit of your goal more enjoyable, and to eliminate obstacles that might hold you back from success.

Remember:

- You're a champion every day and in every way. You know it and every one around you knows it.

- Today, nothing can stand in your way.

- When you need extra determination, you've got it!

- When you need more energy and drive, you've got it!

- You've got the power to get anything done and the patience to overcome challenges, no matter what they may be

- You can do this and you know you can!

MONDAY NUMBER 34

Outcome independence is a powerful, complex concept people seem to have a hard time coming to terms with.

But to me outcome independence means that you're focused more on the actions of achieving the goal than on the progress itself. If your goal is to be physically fit, you should be willing to exercise even if you don't see any progress. You're **independent of the outcome** since you find joy just in the process.

I wrote earlier about making your effort the basis of your progress measurement rather than the results. I explained that the effort is totally within your control, while the results also include elements likely to be out of your control.

It's been said that Thomas Edison endured more than 10,000 failures before he successfully developed a commercially marketable light bulb. That's an astounding number of failures. So it would be reasonably safe to say it's beyond mere mortals' skills to have attempted such feat.

But it's true only if you evaluate the results along the way. If you evaluate the 10,000 attempts as effort and you're measuring effort, then you've become outcome independent. And it's that OI that allows you to make the 10,000 attempts in the first place.

It's important to understand that Edison wanted to create a commercial light bulb and he never lost sight of that goal. He didn't just look at the result of each attempt to determine his progress toward the goal, and he didn't blindly make 10,000 attempts. He took the result of each attempt and used it as feedback to make corrections before making another attempt. And each failure got him closer to his success.

Also keep in mind Jim Rohn's adage: "You should aim to be a millionaire not for the money, but for the person you'll become in the process."

Olympians who don't win gold medals aren't failures, because in the process of going for the gold they became Olympians. They became the type of people who understand the true meaning of discipline and success. They became a lot of great things because they aimed so high.

That alone should be enough for you to become outcome independent, and to focus on building the strength necessary to achieve your goals rather than just being focused on the goal itself.

Of course it doesn't hurt to desire your goal so much so that it ignites a spark of passion. But you should also see the value present in merely pursuing a goal.

And on those tough days where you seem so far from success that you feel like quitting, remind yourself of the person you're becoming by **not** quitting. That's the person you want to become regardless of outcome. You'll become a person who will go through life with more confidence, strength, and resolve than ever before.

That's the kind of person you can be this week!

Exercise 34: Identify Why You're Pursuing Your Goal

Pull out your journal and make a list of reasons why you're pursuing your goal. Then make a separate list of things you love about the pursuit, and the things you see changing about yourself regardless of whether or not you hit the numbers.

Your list may look like this:

- I thought I was doing this just to lose 30 pounds because I want to look great. Even though I've only lost 10 pounds thus far, I feel good about myself because I am now more physically fit and strong, and I love the fact that I can call myself an athlete. I will continue to enjoy working out and how I feel about myself as an athlete even if I never lose all 30 pounds.

- I thought I was writing a novel because I wanted to see my book on a shelf at Barnes and Nobel. I now realize I love writing just for the sake of writing. And getting words on the page, telling stories, and exploring ideas to communicate with a reader in beautiful and compelling ways.

- I thought I was learning how to play the guitar and sing because I wanted to be famous some day. Now I realize that I love practicing my craft even when alone and expressing myself through music.

- I thought I was starting a side business so I could quit my job some day and be my own boss. I now realize that I enjoy the creativity and challenge of running my own business. And I will enjoy working on it even if it never grows large enough to fully support me.

Be sure to read over your list each night before you go to bed, reminding yourself that the process is as important as the end goal.

Remember:

- You're a champion every day and in every way. You know it and every one around you knows it.

- Today, nothing can stand in your way.

- When you need extra determination, you've got it!

- When you need more energy and drive, you've got it!

- You've got the power to get anything done and the patience to overcome challenges, no matter what they may be.

- You can do this and you know you can!

MONDAY
NUMBER 35

How do you build a pyramid? Easy. One stone at a time. Many people are so focused on the outcome of their effort that they forget just how necessary the effort itself is. If you want to build a pyramid, it **is** as simple as building it one stone at a time.

But how many people actually live this philosophy? How many people focus on the day's work instead of getting themselves all torn up about what needs to be accomplished by tomorrow or next week, or how much better they could do if they put off their work until a more appropriate time?

Forget all that. This year is all about doing the work required of you today and nothing more. Of course this could be a lot of work, particularly if you have a lot of goals. But if you constantly fret over how much work you're doing without seeing big results, it may be time to become less results-oriented.

Let's say you've been working on a piece of sculpture, and progress is turtle slow because every day you step back and view it up close. You view it from far away. You view it from every angle possible. But unless you're using that view to give you an idea on what next step you need to take, it's not a very productive activity and the sculpture will take forever to get done.

Imagine how long it might have taken the Egyptians to build the pyramids if they had constantly stood back to look at their work. They might still be trudging through one stone at a time!

In the days before gasoline engines, mules and oxen were used to pull plows through the fields. It was easy to spot the rookie muleskinner who drove the mules, as they constantly looked back to inspect the progress they'd made, rather than waiting until they got to the end of the row. The mules would step out of the row, pulling the plow and a disgruntled muleskinner along with them across neighboring rows.

Sure, you want to calibrate what you're doing with the goal you have in mind. But if you've been doing too much calibration and it's been leading to frustration – well, it's time to eliminate it as it's blocking your progress.

While you want to be focused on being in harmony with your end goal, you can't escape the reality that what you do on a daily basis is equally important. You have to keep chopping at the tree if you want it to fall down. Standing back to watch how much it's leaning isn't going to get you anywhere.

So for this week you're to focus on the art of **just living** on a day-to-day basis. That's all you'll need to worry about. Easy peasy. Even if you believe it's important to "recalibrate" your strategy every once in a while, keep in mind that these are **long-term** strategies you need to focus on.

A day's work is just that: a day's work. If you can't handle that without wondering how far you've come, you're making the journey more difficult than it has to be. So put that stone down, relax, and enjoy the journey while building *your* pyramid!

Exercise 35: Identify One Stone to Put in to Place Each Day

Dig out your calendar, evaluate this week's schedule, and choose one item to tackle each day. Depending on your schedule, these action items can be big or small. The point is to take action toward your goal – even if it's tiny – each day.

Write your actions on the calendar and mark them off each day. Report in to your accountability partner or group to help you follow through.

Remember:

- You're a champion every day and in every way. You know it and every one around you knows it.

- Today, nothing can stand in your way.

- When you need extra determination, you've got it!

- When you need more energy and drive, you've got it!

- You've got the power to get anything done and the patience to overcome challenges, no matter what they may be

- You can do this and you know you can!

MONDAY
NUMBER 36

When was the last time you tried your goal on for size? Let's say you want to buy a car. When's the last time you took a test drive? Or your goal is to win a promotion. When was the last time you got bought new work attire? Or your goal is to buy a new house. When was the last time you looked through advertisements or an online MLS for and went to an open house?

Preparing yourself to achieve your goals can be fun to get lost in the fantasy. The only the difference is, you're actively working on making this fantasy become a reality.

I once knew a fledgling speaker who'd go into an empty auditorium after a big event and have his picture taken on the stage. He'd plant a picture in his subconscious of seats full with people clapping wildly for his stellar presentation. (It should be no surprise that he eventually accomplished his goal.)

Whatever your goal is, find a way to put it in physical terms and try it on for size. Even if it's initially uncomfortable, you'll be wearing it like a pair of Italian loafers before you know it!

Here are a few examples of physical goals:

- Dieters: Go to a store and buy a shirt, pants or dress you plan on fitting into and hang it somewhere you'll see it every day.

- Money savers: Go to the ATM every once in a while and request a balance statement. Then take that statement, cross out the balance, and write what you prefer it to say.

- Actors: Use the "stage" technique you read about above. Imagine an audience completely enthralled with watching you act

- Writers: Take several inches of paper and feel the weight of your "novel" before you even write it.

You should be able to find a physical item you can use to "try on" your own goal for size.

Will this exercise make your goal automatically come to you? Of course it won't. But it's a great way to supercharge your desire, and keep reminding yourself as to why you're putting in all this hard work and effort.

Exercise 36: Test Drive Your Dreams

This week you're to find a scenario to pretend you've already succeeded. Try out any of the following suggestions:

- Ask a friend who works in your desired field if you can shadow them one day at work.

- Ask a successful writer if you can attend a book signing with them. Or if you can exchange pages for critiquing.

- Get someone to take photos of you, keeping only the pictures that are flattering and show off how much you've improved your appearance.

- Buy those jeans you want in a desired size.

- Ask an established artist if you can spend a day in the studio with them. Or help pour molds, set up for an art show, or prep for a major project.

- Audition for a role in a play or band.

- Test drive a new car you plan on buying once you pay down your debt or get that new job.

- Choose the vacation home you're going to rent to celebrate your new business becoming profitable.

Whatever you do this week, physically get out there and practice having succeeded. Don't just think about it – live the part and enjoy the anticipation!

Remember:

- You're a champion every day and in every way. You know it and every one around you knows it.

- Today, nothing can stand in your way.

- When you need extra determination, you've got it!

- When you need more energy and drive, you've got it!

- You've got the power to get anything done and the patience to overcome challenges, no matter what they may be

- You can do this and you know you can!

MONDAY 37
NUMBER

There's a very popular saying in the athletic world: "No pain, no gain." Which implies that you're probably going to be uncomfortable on the road to winning, and that changing yourself for the better often means traveling to uncomfortable places. It's similar to the concept that change is difficult because you're both the sculptor and the sculpture.

One could argue that "no pain, no gain" works well in just about any field. Change is rarely easy. People are afraid to rock the boat, and in many cases their brains are hardwired to want things to remain the same.

Many times the discomfort of change is a result of doing something for the first time. People are afraid of the unknown, so they get anxious over something they've never done before.

Sometimes that discomfort is a result of stretching your limits, and by that very definition it means you're required to step outside your comfort zone. You can never grow beyond your present status without being willing to do what you have never done before.

Eleanor Roosevelt used to say, "Do one thing every day that scares you."

You can turbo charge your journey to your goal by learning to love the space outside your comfort zone. Once you're comfortable with being uncomfortable, you're never going to feel like your attempts to reach your goals are painful. In fact, you'll start to feel lethargic and complacent (there's that pesky word again) if you don't step outside your comfort zone. Something will feel "off," and you'll know somewhere deep inside that there's more to life than what you're currently doing.

Exercise 37: Choose Your Pain

This week you're to take at least one step out of your comfort zone every day. It doesn't have to be anything major. If you're working on your social skills, the first day might be as simple as going for a walk with the goal of saying "hello" to someone. If you're an introvert this could feel a bit overwhelming, so you can start indoors by cold-calling a stranger.

- Meet with a lawyer about establishing your LLC.

- Set up your business bookkeeping software.

- Give up cable and to use the money to hire a mentor.

- File for your divorce so you can be free to date.

- Register for an expensive dating class or a singles mixer.

- Sign up for a marathon training, or a boot camp class that meets at six in the morning.

- Meet with a nutritionist and surrender to an expert.

Do something this week that's painful to do, but has been standing in the way of accomplishing your goal. Remember that it's okay to start small. You don't have to rob a bank just because it's scary. But it doesn't mean you should do something so small that it doesn't scare you at all.

Once you're done, celebrate your victory. Only you know how difficult this was to accomplish, and only you can understand the significance of your choice.

Remember:

- You're a champion every day and in every way. You know it and every one around you knows it.

- Today, nothing can stand in your way.

- When you need extra determination, you've got it!

- When you need more energy and drive, you've got it!

- You've got the power to get anything done and the patience to overcome challenges, no matter what they may be

- You can do this and you know you can!

MONDAY
NUMBER 38

Hopefully at this point in the year your hope for the future hasn't dimmed. You should have some results to show for your efforts, even if you're not quite at the level you want to be at.

Why do I bring this up? Because this week the focus is on gratitude. Yes, **gratitude**. Even though you're only 38 weeks into the year (a great achievement, no doubt, but you're not there yet!), you're going to want to cultivate a habit of being grateful for all the things in your life.

Yes, you have plenty to be grateful for. If you're reading this on your own computer, you can say you have one more computer than many people in the world.

Do you have running water in your house? Are you able to wash your clothes in a washer and dryer, even if it means going down to the local laundromat? Are you free of malaria, a bad case of flu, or a disease that could completely hamper your quality of life?

If you're 10 pounds overweight, be grateful that you're not 20 pounds overweight. If you're 20 pounds overweight, be grateful that you're not 40 and so on.

There's always something to be grateful for. It reminds me of the hilarious scene from the movie "Young Frankenstein," when both Frankenstein and his assistant Igor (pronounced

"Eye-gore," as those of you who have seen the film can attest) are grave-digging for a body and have the following exchange:

Frankenstein: *What a filthy job! (as he shakes goop from his hand)*
Igor: *Could be worse.*
Frankenstein: *How?*
Igor: *Could be raining.*

Of course, after a crash of thunder it immediately starts raining, and Igor sinks into the grave in embarrassment.

But the point is it (whatever "it" is) could be worse. There's always something that's worth being grateful for. It's important to start focusing on what you *do* have today. Because if you can't appreciate what you do have, how do you expect to appreciate your goal once you've achieved it?

Remember Jim Rohn's statement about becoming a millionaire not for the money, but for the person you'll become? Well, this may sound strange. But by the time you reach your goal, there's a good chance it won't be as big a deal to you as it was in the beginning. Part of the nature of growth is you get used to bigger and better things.

So practice being grateful *now*, because this habit will help you to live a more cheerful, happy life. It will help you to be happy even when the odds are stacked against you.

This week you're to wake up every day with a smile on your face, and be grateful the earth didn't stop spinning on its axis. That is, after all, just another thing to be grateful for.

Exercise 38: Give to Someone Less Fortunate

Identify someone who's less fortunate than you, and determine what you can do this week to make their life better. As you give to this person (raking an elderly neighbor's leaves or paying for a friend's lunch), remind yourself of how lucky you are that you're able to give in this way.

If you don't know anyone who needs a hand, find a charitable organization and volunteer, or perform a random act of kindness. This will be most effective if your act of generosity requires time and effort, and if you get to see how this person benefits from your charitable act.

If possible, tie your act of generosity to your end goal. For example, if your goal is to lose weight, raking leaves is a perfect way to exercise and serve your neighbor at the same time. If your goal is to write a book, you could volunteer at your child's school by reading aloud to their class or sign up to mentor a child.

If you want to start a photography business, you could donate your services to the Humane Society for an afternoon and take photos of animals that need to be adopted. If your goal is to meet a life partner, volunteer somewhere you imagine your future partner might be. All the while you should keep your focus on how lucky you are to be able to pursue your goals.

Remember:

- You're a champion every day and in every way. You know it and every one around you knows it.

- Today, nothing can stand in your way.

- When you need extra determination, you've got it!

- When you need more energy and drive, you've got it!

- You've got the power to get anything done and the patience to overcome challenges, no matter what they may be

- You can do this and you know you can!

MONDAY NUMBER 39

This week is all about cultivating a healthy obsession. Now, that term might strike you as something of an oxymoron – like saying "dry rain" or "happy frown." But there's a secret few people know: The concept of healthy obsession *does* exist.

Think about your neighbor who used to go on ten mile runs every morning no matter what the weather was. "He's obsessed!" you'd probably say. But you'd be hard pressed to deny that he was in really good shape.

This week you're to remember a time when you had a healthy obsession. Perhaps it was the first time you fell in love. At first it meant you were totally enamored with them. You spent all your free time with them. And when you weren't together, you thought about the next time you'd be together and how long the relationship would last. Maybe you wrote their name a hundred times in a notebook. You were, in a word, obsessed.

Not being obsessed with your main goal may be the reason you're having problems progressing. Along those same lines, if you've been "dating" the goal for a while and you're not sure the chemistry is there and your passion has failed to ignite, it may be time to move on and select another goal more to your liking. It's okay to "break up" with your goal and leave it on an amicable basis.

If on the other hand your initial obsession with your goal has moved on to a more mature relationship, it's time to step on the gas and renew the earlier passion you had. Now is the time to draw on your initial energy and to once again seize the day. *Carpe diem*, y'all!

Love, as you know, is a powerful emotion. And it's just as powerful while seeking your goals as it is in your relationships. Once you understand that it's okay to have a healthy obsession, you'll start to see the level of desire it takes to achieve success.

This week you're to focus on rekindling the passion you had for your goal at the beginning of the year. Or when you reconsidered your goal later on and it inspired you to continue. Think back to that moment and ask yourself how you can get back into that mindset.

Here's a hint: Energy flows where your focus is pointed (remembering me mentioning "due north"?) The more you focus on something, the more you'll think about it, and the more obsessed you'll become.

Exercise 39: Get Caught Up In Your Obsession

This week you need to find a group of people even more obsessed with your goal than you are and spend time with them. You should already have an accountability partner, one or more groups you've participated in, or an online forum of some sort. Sift through these resources to find a local meeting of like-minded people and join them for a motivational experience.

For example, you might do one of the following:

- Attend a film festival or a Meet Up of aspiring filmmakers.

- Attend a weekend long weight loss or fitness group session.

- Go to a book fair or art fair.

- Drop in on a trade show or convention.

- Sign up for an instructional session on dating, or a speed dating event.

When you go to an event, think of yourself as a story collector. Talk to as many people as possible about why they started pursuing their goal and how it's gone for them so far. If possible attend a motivational speech. Afterwards, see if you can talk to the speaker for a few moments and ask them the same question. Let yourself get carried along by the enthusiasm of the group setting.

Remember:

- You're a champion every day and in every way. You know it and every one around you knows it.

- Today, nothing can stand in your way.

- When you need extra determination, you've got it!

- When you need more energy and drive, you've got it!

- You've got the power to get anything done and the patience to overcome challenges, no matter what they may be

- You can do this and you know you can!

MONDAY *40*
NUMBER

Two things to learn this week: 1) You can find inspiration anywhere, and 2) there are always people who want to burst your bubble.

I once saw a top-ranked high school football recruit being interviewed. When the reporter asked him about his favorite movie, he said that it was in fact Disney's "The Lion King." The reporter was taken aback, and cynically asked him what he could possibly see in what's essentially a kid's movie (obviously forgetting that even 18-year-olds can still be young at heart).

The recruit replied that he had learned a lot of life lessons from "The Lion King" and it helped him to set goals. Even though he gave a passionate, intelligent response, the reporter quickly changed the subject rather than to explore it further.

The moral of the story? Regardless of who you are and what you're aiming to achieve, there will always be naysayers who might not agree with your methods. Maybe they think you train funny, or that your idea of an inspiring movie is childish.

But that's okay. You have one life to live, so you should feel comfortable finding inspiration wherever it can be found. If something has meaning to you, that's all that matters.

In fact, even if you find profound inspiration in things that are "corny" or "hokey," you should feel perfectly comfortable there as well. When the interview was over, the recruit said to the surprised reporter: "Hakuna Matata! [No worries]."

You don't have to worry about what other people think. Their bad attitudes aren't getting them anywhere, and there's a good chance they secretly wish they could find the same amount of passion in their lives as you display in yours.

Instead of worrying about what people will think about your passions and inspirations, be proud of them. Wear them on your sleeve. After all, if you don't allow yourself to be inspired, how can you ever inspire anyone else?

Exercise 40: Find Your Inspiration

This week you're going to fully embrace that video clip, music, poster, movie, concert, museum – whatever it is that inspires you – and make it more prominent in your life.

Be open about your passions to whoever is willing to listen. You may end up inspiring them and yourself as a bonus. Email that marketing guru, or plaster that slogan all over your apartment. Devote an entire evening to immersing yourself in the inspiration that comes from an art form or someone else's success.

Each morning before you start your day play a few bars of that song, watch a minute of that video clip, or spend a moment gazing at that poster and dreaming about how one day you'll succeed.

Remember:

- You're a champion every day and in every way. You know it and every one around you knows it.

- Today, nothing can stand in your way.

- When you need extra determination, you've got it!

- When you need more energy and drive, you've got it!

- You've got the power to get anything done and the patience to overcome challenges, no matter what they may be

- You can do this and you know you can!

MONDAY
NUMBER *41*

If you've ever been to a high school football game, you're probably familiar with a tradition similar to baseball's seventh inning stretch but with a little twist. This tradition takes place between the third and fourth quarters just as the last period of the game is about to take place. Everyone on the team raises their hands with four fingers extended, signifying that the fourth quarter is upon them. But they don't raise their fingers like that for any other quarter, since the fourth quarter is the most important.

As you enter the fourth quarter of your 52-month commitment, I hope you've got your hand thrust proud and high into the air with four fingers extended. I hope you're telling yourself that you've got 90 days left to make something great happen this year. And that those 90 days might be more crucial than any other that happened earlier in the year.

Like a long-distance runner you know that now is the time to increase the energy in your stride. It's time to focus on what you want and eye your goal like a hawk eyeing its prey, knowing that you're about to go after it full speed with everything you have.

Three months left means you still have plenty to accomplish. This isn't the last week of the year, but now that you've come this far you know what can be done and you're not going to waste the next 90 days. So extend those four fingers to say you're going to make the most out of the fourth quarter.

One thing that has always fascinated me is the fact that many teams always perform this fourth quarter ritual no matter how far down they may be, or how much they're ahead of the other team. The message they're sending is that the fourth quarter is important because the other team could stage a comeback. And that they have rededicated themselves to the game because they know the fourth quarter is when it could all slip away.

In other words, put those fingers up no matter how far you've come even if you haven't come all that far. This is the only life you get. This **is not** a dress rehearsal! You're in the game and you're in the fourth quarter. Are you ready for your touchdown?

Exercise 41: Take on a New Habit

You've seen the power of establishing new habits. Maybe you decided to drink a glass of water before every meal, or say your affirmations in the mirror each morning. Perhaps you committed to smiling at every person you meet, or to doing 30 sit-ups every night before bed.

Now it's time to pick your fourth quarter habit. Have coffee with your accountability partner and choose your habit together. Talk through the rewards and consequences for sticking with it or breaking it.

Commit to your fourth quarter habit on paper, on your calendar, in your journal and online. Then hit the ground running and practice your daily habit with conviction.

Remember:

- You're a champion every day and in every way. You know it and every one around you knows it.

- Today, nothing can stand in your way.

- When you need extra determination, you've got it!

- When you need more energy and drive, you've got it!

- You've got the power to get anything done and the patience to overcome challenges, no matter what they may be

- You can do this and you know you can!

MONDAY
NUMBER 42

This week is about learning how to say no. "Just say no!" was a phrase made famous by an anti-drug campaign in the 1980s. But it's also an action that can make you a lot more focused and ready to achieve your goals.

How this happens isn't immediately obvious. You go through your day constantly influenced by external factors, the most powerful of which is other people – their words, expectations, mannerisms, and how they feel about what you're doing.

Many people (could this be you?) go about their lives as people pleasers. They believe that it's more important to please others (since they want to be seen as a good person) than to achieve their own goals, which is a very limited view of the real meaning behind "achieving a goal."

But you're allowed to say no to people. You're allowed to decline invitations. You're allowed to cancel commitments. You're allowed to place your goals first in your list of priorities to a reasonable extent.

But I'd argue that "reasonable extent" goes much further than most people are aware.

You see, it's better to be vigilant against the many influencing factors in your life and place your goals as a high priority than to be a people pleaser.

Why? Because ultimately you can't please all people. And few people respect someone who doesn't have their own set of priorities. In fact, it's not normal to always say yes; it's normal to say no when they're asking you to do something that violates your standards.

This approach has caused me to miss some pretty interesting opportunities, like the chance to play golf with one of my favorite actor/comedians, Bill Murray. But it's also made me more effective at goal achievement been since I place my actions high on the list of my priorities, and allow the rest of life to follow suit.

If you want to make yourself a priority, you're going to have to reject people's negative behavior. If they criticize or mock you for how you're behaving, then ditch them. They're not supportive enough to be a true friend, and they'll ultimately try to bring you down once you reach your goals.

"No" may be a negative word, but that doesn't mean it can't be used to affect positive change in your life. So this week you're to make sure it's used positively, and that you're placing your goals high on your list of priorities. After your closest friends and family, let other engagements fall by the wayside. You have to practice being **you** before you can help others.

Exercise 42: Eliminate Distractions

Evaluate your upcoming week. What extra commitments have you allowed to creep back into your life?

Cancel everything that gets in the way, and devote at least one entire evening (or better yet one entire weekend) to working on your goal.

If someone challenges you, explain how important your goal is. If that's not appropriate, just say "Something personal came up." You really don't owe them an explanation, but you do owe the time to yourself.

So what will you do with that extra time? That's up to you, but you'll want to make it count. Give your goal a fighting chance this week by giving enough time to the process.

Remember:

- You're a champion every day and in every way. You know it and every one around you knows it.

- Today, nothing can stand in your way.

- When you need extra determination, you've got it!

- When you need more energy and drive, you've got it!

- You've got the power to get anything done and the patience to overcome challenges, no matter what they may be.

- You can do this and you know you can!

MONDAY
NUMBER 43

Have you ever heard of a "clutch" performer? You'd be surprised, but many great athletes of our time were great clutch performers in that they rose to the occasion when the pressure was highest and their nerves could have otherwise gotten the best of them.

For example, NBA great Michael Jordan – widely considered the greatest basketball player of all time – is remembered for scoring a ton of points and being a star during a regular season, right? Wrong. He's remembered because of his clutch performances, and his ability to dial his skills to another level when his team needed him the most. People remember Michael Jordan for hitting last-minute shots to win championships. People remember him as a clutch performer.

There is an assuredness to clutch performers that's interesting to watch. They move as if they know that somehow, some way they're going to end up winning the game. It's almost as if the art of being a clutch performer is simply having a strong belief in yourself…and that's it.

Of course, that's a fallacy. Michael Jordan was great because he was fearlessly competitive, an insanely hard worker, was genetically gifted, and was obsessed with winning.

There are a lot of hard workers who may be genetically gifted and never seem to rise to the heights of a clutch performer. So why is it that some succeed and some fail? The truth is a clutch performer has a very clear standard in mind. They know what needs to be done and they're willing to take action to make sure it gets done. While they're thinking about what they can do to win a game, the other team is letting their nerves get to them and imagining how they'll feel if they fail in the most crucial moments.

Whose attitude do you think is going to succeed nine out of ten times? Obviously, the clutch performer; the player who's thinking about what needs to be done and has the confidence to feel they'll ultimately be successful. In the end, it's essentially a self-fulfilling prophecy.

Now is not the time to worry that you don't have enough time left. Champions always have enough time because they make the most of it. Now is the time to take your effort to the next level, operating with the full confidence that your highly focused work will produce a last minute win. Now is the time for you to become a clutch performer.

What if I fail? you might ask yourself (that's the kind of self-doubt you shouldn't allow into your mind). Remember that even Michael Jordan missed a lot of last minute shots, but he never gave up. When you know you can always come back after a bad clutch performance, you're free to perform at your best. It's coming down to crunch time for the rest of the year. So how do you think you'll react?

Exercise 43: Double Down

This week's exercise is to evaluate your last 42 weeks, and identify which week was the most exciting and effective. Now you're to replicate that week's efforts and push for even greater movement going forward into the rest of the year.

When you finish this week, journal about what made it so effective. Then make this week the blueprint for future successful weeks. Why reinvent the wheel when you've already figured out what helps you move the ball forward?

Remember:

- You're a champion every day and in every way. You know it and every one around you knows it.

- Today, nothing can stand in your way.

- When you need extra determination, you've got it!

- When you need more energy and drive, you've got it!

- You've got the power to get anything done and the patience to overcome challenges, no matter what they may be

- You can do this and you know you can!

MONDAY
NUMBER 44

What do you do with your idle time? For many people their idle time isn't idle at all; it's instead a highly influential time that helps determine what their predominant attitude will be throughout the day.

For instance, maybe you believe strongly in the power of autosuggestion. So you repeat your affirmations every morning and every evening with as much feeling, faith, and self-confidence as you can muster. But the results don't show up.

What's going on?

In this case, it might be that your autosuggestion is just fine; it's the suggestions you make to yourself during your idle time that counteract your results.

For example, you want to submit an article to a magazine as part of your goal to become a writer. You write for 15 minutes and feel good about yourself. But then you decide to go wash the dishes. During this "idle" time your mind starts churning about all the reasons you might fail. You start feeling like your work isn't adequate, and that your efforts are pointless because no one will ever accept your article for publication. In this case you're not just writing and doing the dishes: You're writing, doing the dishes, and working against yourself by not using your idle time in a more positive way.

It's important to recognize that autosuggestions happen all the time. All your thoughts – and not just the thoughts you purposefully plant in your mind – become your actions.

So how can you change this to ensure you're living in a healthier and more productive atmosphere conducive to a more positive attitude? It's simple. You need to find ways to feel better about yourself during your idle time. For example, watching TV while playing chess online to feel stimulated. Playing inspiring music while you're doing the dishes. Using idle time in the car to listen to an inspiring audio. Or making positive affirmations about the success you see yourself receiving one day.

Yes, it will take discipline to see this through. But you don't have to do a lot of work to create a better environment for yourself. You just need to focus on being happier, and you'll find that many autosuggestions are that much more effective. In short, practice the habit of being happy by using your idle time in much smarter ways.

Exercise 44: Fill the Void with Positive Energy

This week you're to listen to a podcast, webinar or an audiobook, or read about someone who has succeeded in a situation that inspires you. Fill your idle time with stories that feed your "I can" spirit.

Before you go to bed each night, jot down one line from the material that inspired you. Then reread it when you get up each morning to keep that epiphany top-of-mind.

Remember:

- You're a champion every day and in every way. You know it and every one around you knows it.

- Today, nothing can stand in your way.

- When you need extra determination, you've got it!

- When you need more energy and drive, you've got it!

- You've got the power to get anything done and the patience to overcome challenges, no matter what they may be

- You can do this and you know you can!

MONDAY
NUMBER 45

Fall is the time of year for a daylight savings shift. When you set your clock back one hour you essentially "gain" one hour of time. This is an interesting concept, because it allows people to do something with that extra hour of time.

Many people use it to sleep, because they know the extra hour usually arrives in the middle of the night. They use the hour to sleep in and feel a little more refreshed the next day. There's nothing wrong with a good night's sleep. But when you get **one** chance per year to repeat an hour, isn't there something a little nobler you could do with your time?

The point to all of this is *you can do that all the time*. Picture this: What if you had one extra hour where you could focus exclusively on your goals?

The truth is many people wouldn't use that hour to work on their goals, but would find a way to fill it with something noncommittal. They'd rather sleep in, watch a late night movie, gab with a friend, or play an online game rather than working on something to get them closer to their goal. They fritter away valuable time they'll never get back.

Most goal setting experts agree that even a tiny degree increase in efforts would double, triple, and even quadruple people's efforts over the long haul (it's just like making an extra deposit into an interest-bearing bank account every year).

So where do you find that extra hour? It's simple: Twelve minutes per day for five work days is all it takes to get one extra hour of time per week. **Twelve measly minutes!** Since this is a guide on 52 Mondays, one extra hour spent each week toward your goal is 52 hours per year you can use to achieve success. That's 60 minutes per day, or 3,120 minutes extra per year to realize your dream.

People reason it can't be that easy, which is why they don't immediately adopt this new habit of devoting one extra hour to their goal. They're so focused on immediate gratification that they're unwilling to see the big picture of working on their goal 12 extra minutes a day. They'd rather work hard, burn out, and give up before they've achieved success. But that's **not** how you're going to live your life. So this week you're going to study your daily habits and find 12 minutes every day you can move from the time wasted column into the goal achievement column. Are you spending 12 minutes dawdling in the shower that could be used to brainstorm ideas? Are you driving to work and not using 12 minutes to listen to an expert talk about starting a new business?

When you start thinking about time this way, the world will open itself up to you. If you become more proactive about your time, you may find that 24 hours in a day is more than enough to live the life of your dreams if it's used wisely.

Exercise 45: Use Your 12 Minutes Wisely!

Identify something you can do for 12 minutes each day that will get you closer to your goal. For example, in 12 minutes you can:

- Write and post a blogpost on your website.

- Email a current or potential client to about their needs.

- Run a mile (or further).

- Complete a conditioning circuit.

- Write 500 words of a screenplay, novel, or magazine article.

- Edit something you've already written.

- Practice a musical piece three times.

- Sketch.

- Follow up with a person of interest you met at a social gathering.

- Meditate to release stress.

- Stretch to get your blood flowing and endorphins running.

Choose something to do for 12 minutes each day, and focus 100% on your goal as you perform it. Make the most of your 12 minutes each day!

Remember:

- You're a champion every day and in every way. You know it and every one around you knows it.

- Today, nothing can stand in your way.

- When you need extra determination, you've got it!

- When you need more energy and drive, you've got it!

- You've got the power to get anything done and the patience to overcome challenges, no matter what they may be

- You can do this and you know you can!

MONDAY
NUMBER 46

I'd like to use an example from the game of football to remember the importance of giving everything you have. There's a situation known as **fourth and goal**, which is the offense's last chance to score a touchdown. They're too close to the end zone to get a first down before they have to give the ball to the other team.

Some teams will go for the touchdown. Some teams will take a more subtle approach and go for a touchdown only if they think they can get it. Other teams will play it more conservative and take the three points of a field goal. It's fewer points, but there's also less chance of having scored nothing and giving the other team the ball.

As you come to the end of your 52 Mondays, remember this analogy of fourth and goal. Are you going for the touchdown? Or are you going to settle for the field goal? The correct way to assess the situation is to examine what your momentum is like at the current moment. Some coaches who know their running game has been effective will run the ball on fourth and goal, trusting the momentum will continue. What does your momentum up to now say about what your strategy should be for the next few weeks? Baseball icon Yogi Berra's sage advice was "It ain't over 'til it's over."

Exercise 46: Setting Yourself Up to Score

Your exercise is to evaluate what it will take to reach your goal at the end of the year. Is it within reach? What do you need to do to make that happen? You need to map out the rest of the year, detailing what risks you'll need to take in order to make this happen. If your goal is out of reach, reset it for the end of the year so it is attainable. Then map out your plan from today until the end of the year.

Be sure to plan one or more action items for the remaining six weeks such as working out more, planning your meals more regularly, etc. Plan your weeks so you achieve your action item at the beginning of each one so that you have time to catch up if you get behind. Make sure your accountability partner sees your plan for the remainder of the year and knows what you action items are.

Remember:

- You're a champion every day and in every way. You know it and every one around you knows it.

- Today, nothing can stand in your way.

- When you need extra determination, you've got it!

- When you need more energy and drive, you've got it!

- You've got the power to get anything done and the patience to overcome challenges, no matter what they may be

- You can do this and you know you can!

MONDAY
NUMBER *47*

For Americans, November is the month for Thanksgiving. You see ads everywhere talking about Thanksgiving specials. Television series have their Thanksgiving episodes. Teachers assign homework that asks their students to write what they're thankful for.

But you don't have to live in the United States to recognize the importance of being thankful. A previous chapter looked at gratitude and its importance to your goal, and noted just how powerful being grateful can be. If you can't be happy now, who's to say that achieving your goal will automatically change your happiness in the future?

Well, I do. You should be dedicating time every day to think of all the things you have to be thankful for. Many studies show that people who regularly count their blessings are generally happier, healthier and more successful than those who tend to focus on what they don't have.

For the rest of this month you're to put a notebook you've titled "Gratitude" on your nightstand. Before going to bed you're going to record at least five things you're grateful for. Sometimes you'll think about big things, like the people in your life. Other times you may be thankful that someone invented deep dish pizza. Whatever you're thankful for, write it down every single day. Then when Thanksgiving rolls around and people ask you what you're thankful for, you'll know what to tell them.

Trust me: Before the month is out you'll notice a subtle shift in your life and you'll just seem to attract things. Coincidence? I don't think so.

Exercise 47: Record Your Blessings

Write five things you're grateful for in your Gratitude notebook each night before you go to bed. Look for blessings that feed your goal, and help you remain motivated and inspired. Want to turbo-charge this? Read your gratitude list out loud each morning before you start your day. Thank friends, co-workers, neighbors and family whenever you notice someone doing something kind or positive for you.

Remember:

- You're a champion every day and in every way. You know it and every one around you knows it.

- Today, nothing can stand in your way.

- When you need extra determination, you've got it!

- When you need more energy and drive, you've got it!

- You've got the power to get anything done and the patience to overcome challenges, no matter what they may be

- You can do this and you know you can!

MONDAY

I'm going to devote a second week to developing an attitude of gratitude. But this time you're going to think about the people in your life who have made a positive impact. After you take time to think about it, you'll realize there are a lot more people than you might have realized.

If you've been keeping a Gratitude journal, you should get it out. If not, start a new one. (Hey, why didn't you listen to me last week? Tsk-tsk.)

List at least five people you're grateful for. Every day this week, take time to send a card or letter (an actual physical piece of paper and not an email!) to each of the people on your list, and tell them you're thankful that they're in your life. Get specific about the impact they've had on you and speak genuinely from the heart.

When I first did this exercise my list included my stepfather, my high school coach, and a priest who had a huge impact on my life. Today I can vividly recall my feelings as I wrote each of them, even though it was several years ago. Years later when my coach died of cancer, I was extremely grateful that I'd taken the opportunity to let him know how he had blessed my life in such a monumental way.

As Jim Rohn said (and I keep reminding you), strive to be a success because of the person you will become along the way. This exercise is one example of how true that can be.

Exercise 48: Journal About Someone For Whom You're Grateful

This week you're to write in your journal about someone who affected your life in a profound way. Then list all the details of how your success will make you and those around you happier and more well off. Enjoy the positive vibe throughout the week as you pursue your goal.

Remember:

- You're a champion every day and in every way. You know it and every one around you knows it.

- Today, nothing can stand in your way.

- When you need extra determination, you've got it!

- When you need more energy and drive, you've got it!

- You've got the power to get anything done and the patience to overcome challenges, no matter what they may be

- You can do this and you know you can!

MONDAY
NUMBER 49

If your final month for the program is December, it could be tempting to give in to the holidays and wait until January to start again. Now, I've got nothing against holidays. I love being in touch with family, letting the belt get a little looser, and having a good time as everyone remembers just how blessed they are.

But holidays aren't an excuse to throw caution to the wind and forget about your goals.

Remember the chapter about momentum? Well, it said that it's easier to start again if you never let your foot off the gas and keep rolling forward. That's what you need to be thinking about as this time rolls around. In fact, if you're close to your goal but not quite there yet, it may be time to think about stepping it up a notch.

Even so, it can't hurt to plan out the rest of the year and into the next, because you certainly won't feel like it at Christmas. Take time this week to focus on how you can still achieve this year's goals while riding that momentum into the New Year.

Don't be afraid to start with a clean slate. You can keep the routines that have been working, but start fresh with your goals. As you readdress your goals, you'll probably find that you're different than at the beginning of the 52 weeks. You're more ambitious. You're more in tune with what kind of plans are required to achieve these goals. You're more in tune with yourself.

Make a pledge that you'll have all your goals and plans in place for next year by the time New Year's Eve comes around. You'll be amazed at how much better you feel and how much you've learned throughout the year. This may be your best holiday season ever!

Exercise 49: Ride Your Momentum

Instead of getting distracted, ride your momentum into the end of the year by stretching yourself to meet your goal. The biggest gift you can give yourself is a holiday victory.

Reach out to people who can give help you meet your goal. Ask a personal trainer for a few extra minutes in the gym, or your nutritionist for delicious low-cal recipes. Invite a business contact or colleague out for lunch or coffee date. Initiate a date with someone you've eyed from afar, and give them a small gift. You'll find your success will be all the sweeter when discovered during the holiday season!

Remember:

- You're a champion every day and in every way. You know it and every one around you knows it.

- Today, nothing can stand in your way.

- When you need extra determination, you've got it!

- When you need more energy and drive, you've got it!

- You've got the power to get anything done and the patience to overcome challenges, no matter what they may be

- You can do this and you know you can!

MONDAY NUMBER 50

In the beautiful book of Ecclesiastes, Solomon in essence says "There's a time to plant or sow in season, another time to pluck or reap."

That's a great thing to think about as you zero in on your goals at the end of the year. All year you've been sowing seeds for success. And if your success has grown from those seeds, you'll know it's the right time to "reap" and enjoy your holidays by cutting yourself some slack (while not taking your foot completely off the pedal).

Perhaps you haven't worked as hard as you could have. In that case, it may be the season to sow more seeds; to get a little ambitious in your goal setting; and to use the holiday season to inspire you to greater growth.

It's impossible to not eventually reap what you sow. It may not come at a time of your choosing, and you may not be sure what the consequences will be. But what you planted yesterday and today will figure into your future.

Your state of mind during the holiday season will give you a little break to think about this premise. You'll see your friends and family, and what they've been reaping (i.e., they're fitter, healthier, happier, etc.) throughout the year.

As you plow your field for another year of work, it's important to know the seeds you've sown this year are still there and are still growing. Don't be surprised if the harvest begins when you least expect it, even if it isn't at the perfect time. What matters is that you will reap well if you have sown well.

Exercise 50: Sow Your Last Seeds of the Year

Conduct your last efforts of the year, which means you should do something along these lines:

- Schedule your weekly workouts in such a way that you're sure to stick to them.

- Plan your meals and shop accordingly.

- Cold call a list of potential clients.

- Write thank you cards to those who have helped you this year (new clients, mentors, advisors, partners, etc.).

- Carve out time for one last extended creative session.

- Submit your work to judges, contests or publications.

- Plan a holiday party with the people you've met over the past year.

Enjoy these last lunges to see if you can make it to your end goal with one mighty push.

Remember:

- You're a champion every day and in every way. You know it and every one around you knows it.

- Today, nothing can stand in your way.

- When you need extra determination, you've got it!

- When you need more energy and drive, you've got it!

- You've got the power to get anything done and the patience to overcome challenges, no matter what they may be

- You can do this and you know you can!

MONDAY NUMBER 51

It's crazy how much holiday advertising you see these days, and yet that's exactly what goes on in the 51st week of the year. Think about all the times you've seen a sign that says "Only 15 Shopping Days Left Till Christmas." This marketing ploy is a great way to get people in a mindset of scarcity, and to believe their time is running out. But if used differently, benchmarks such as these can help you along the path to success.

As you make your new plans for next year, consider using benchmarks to track your progress. For example, if you want to lose 40 pounds next year make sure you set a goal of losing ten pounds every three months (feel free to change the timing to suit your needs and schedule). These "mile markers" along the way to success will ensure that you'll eventually arrive at your end goal, even if the journey takes a little longer than you'd like.

I couldn't let the opportunity slip by to use other examples from the holiday season. What's the highest volume traffic retail shopping day of the year? Black Friday, the day after Thanksgiving. What's the best time to buy decorations and gifts for next Christmas? Right after this Christmas when they go on sale. Well, the best day to start working on next year's goal is the day after the end of this year's goal.

Exercise 51: Plan Next Year's Goals

This week's exercise is to meet with your accountability buddy (if that relationship has deteriorated, ask someone new to commit to pursuing your goal with you. If you can't find an accountability partner, use an online service or some sort of measuring device that allows you to set goals and check off your accomplishments.) Together you can talk through your current accomplishments and plan goals for next year, complete with:

- Measurable goals.

- Benchmarks.

- A list of activities that worked well for you this past year.

- A list of activities that didn't work so well.

- A plan for that first month so you can hit the ground running.

Remember:

- You're a champion every day and in every way. You know it and every one around you knows it.

- Today, nothing can stand in your way.

- When you need extra determination, you've got it!

- When you need more energy and drive, you've got it!

- You've got the power to get anything done and the patience to overcome challenges, no matter what they may be

- You can do this and you know you can!

MONDAY
NUMBER 52

You made it! One year, 52 Mondays, 365 days of accomplishments. I want to congratulate you for making it this far and achieving what you set out to do. **Bravo!**

Your results may be greater or less than you expected. But I hope what you learned is that it's never wrong to persistently take action toward your goal, even if you don't achieve it right away. And just practicing being disciplined is sometimes enough.

If you achieved your goal, great! But if you didn't? That's something left for next year, isn't it? You never stop growing and improving; otherwise, what is life all about? You're not the same person you were last year, thanks to your efforts. You're smarter and wiser. And because of your goal you may be fitter, happier, wealthier and more secure.

I want you to leave Fifty Two Mondays with this thought: Earl Nightingale said that success is the progressive realization of a worthy goal. Not the attainment – **the progressive realization of it**.

As long as you're taking action every day that brings you closer to your goal, no one can call you anything other than what you are: A *go-getter*, a *doer*, a *champion*!

Final Exercise: Celebrate!

Take yourself out for a grand celebration and do it up right! Pull out all the stops. Get all gussied up. Celebrate with your accountability buddy, someone you've met along the way, or your best pal who knows the struggles you've been going through.

Take "after" pictures if you've changed physically, or print out proof that shows how much growth you've had with your particular project. Share stories of overcoming hardship, and laugh about the limitations you used to place on yourself. Most importantly, celebrate how much further along you are because of your 52 weeks of effort.

Remember:

- You're a champion every day and in every way. You know it and every one around you knows it.

- Today, nothing can stand in your way.

- When you need extra determination, you've got it!

- When you need more energy and drive, you've got it!

- You've got the power to get anything done and the patience to overcome challenges, no matter what they may be

- You can do this and you know you can!

CONCLUSION
THE NEXT NEW YEAR

Where do you go from here? It's simple. You start a new year… again…which doesn't have to be a bad thing. If you successfully completed the 52 weeks in this program you should be at the top of your game. Instead of watching another year go by and wondering where all the time went, you finally put time to good use.

That means you have arrived here, at the end, having made a lot of progress. You haven't just progressed toward your goals, but you've actually grown as a person.

As my mentor and friend Jim Rohn said, don't become a millionaire for the money, but for the person you become along the way. That person you've become over the last 52 weeks should understand now what goes into achieving success: Diligence, goal setting, persistence, smart habits, gratitude, and sharing with others. And you should be able to repeat that formula every year for the rest of your life.

It shouldn't be your goal to repeat this year – you want to build on this year's success. Otherwise, the next time 12 months rolls by, what will you have to show for your efforts? You'll be seeing more sand slip through the hourglass while everyone around you seems to be improving their lives.

So what can you do to ensure that you take advantage of the upcoming year? For starters, you should ride the momentum you've gained throughout this year. That means you should use all your knowledge and experience and never stop using it. If you've established some daily habits, keep them up *through* the New Year and into the next. And *don't* let the holidays get in your way.

Then set new goals. Set more ambitious goals. You may have surprised yourself last year by achieving your goals early, so maybe they need some tweaking. Add some steps to your plan, like benchmarks along the way to better track your progress.

As you keep working toward your goals, ask yourself if there are *more* challenges to take on and *more* learning opportunities along the way. You'll be glad you did. After all, in another 52 weeks you'll have to ask yourself the same question: *What did I accomplish this year?*

If you'd like some support and want to be around a group of like-minded people, I suggest checking out TheChampionsClub. org. We'd love to have you join us!

And *always* remember: You're a champion every day and in every way. You know it and every one around you knows it. Today, nothing can stand in your way. When you need extra determination, you've got it! When you need more energy and drive, you've got it! You've got the power to get anything done and the patience to overcome challenges, no matter what they may be. You can do this and you know you can!

Urgent Plea!

Thank you for downloading my master's book! It will really help life around here. Would you please help Vic (and me) and go back to the site where you purchased this book and leave your feedback. He needs your feedback to make the next version better. Arf! Arf!

Other Books from Laurenzana Press

The Strangest Secret by Earl Nightingale

Memory Improvement : How to Improve Your Memory in Just 30 Days by Ron White

Persistence & Perseverance: Dance Until It Rains by The Champions Club

The Law of Attraction: How To Get What You Want by Robert Collier

Time Management Tips: 101 Best Ways to Manage Your Time by Lucas McCain

Get Motivated: 101 Best Ways to Get Started, Keep Going and Finish Strong by Lucas McCain

Successful & Healthy Aging: 101 Best Ways to Feel Younger & Live Longer by Lisa J. Johnson

Self Confidence Secrets: How To Be Outgoing and Overcome Shyness by Lucas McCain

Happiness Habits: 21 Secrets to Living a Fun and Outrageously Rewarding Life by Lucas McCain

Self Help Books: The 101 Best Personal Development Classics by Vic Johnson

Overcoming Fear: 101 Best Ways to Overcome Fear and Anxiety and Take Control of Your Life Today! by Lucas McCain

Public Speaking Fear? 21 Secrets To Succeed In Front of Any Crowd by Lucas McCain

Going Green : 101 Ways To Save A Buck While You Save The Earth by Lucas McCain

Stress Management : 101 Best Ways to Relieve Stress and Really Live Life by Lucas McCain

Should I Divorce? 11 Questions To Answer Before You Decide to Stay or Go by Jennifer Jessica

Divorce Recovery: 101 Best Ways To Cope, Heal And Create A Fabulous Life After a Divorce by Lisa J. Johnson

About The Author

Eleven years ago Vic Johnson was totally unknown in the personal development field. Since that time he's created six of the most popular personal development sites on the Internet. One of them, AsAManthinketh.net has given away over 400,000 copies of James Allen's classic book. Three of them are listed in the top 5% of websites in the world (English language).

This success has come despite the fact that he and his family were evicted from their home sixteen years ago and the next year his last automobile was repossessed. His story of redemption and victory has inspired thousands around the world as he has taught the powerful principles that created incredible wealth in his life and many others.

Today he serves more than 300,000 subscribers from virtually every country in the world. He's become an internationally known expert in goal achieving and hosted his own TV show, Goals 2 Go, on TSTN. His book, *13 Secrets of World Class Achievers,* is the number one goal setting book at both the Kindle store and Apple iBookstore. Another best seller, *Day by Day with James Allen,* has sold more than 75,000 copies and has been translated into Japanese, Czech, Slovak and Farsi. His three-day weekend seminar event, Claim Your Power Now, has attracted such icons as Bob Proctor, Jim Rohn, Denis Waitley and many others.

His websites include:

TheChampionsClub.org
AsAManThinketh.net
Goals2Go.com
MyDailyInsights.com
VicJohnson.com
mp3Motivators.com
ClaimYourPowerNow.com
GettingRichWitheBooks.com
LaurenzanaPress.com

CPSIA information can be obtained at www.ICGtesting.com
Printed in the USA
LVOW011324071212

310600LV00007B/37/P